W R   O K S

£ 14·99/-

Learning Centre
Hayes Community Campus
Coldharbour Lane, Hayes, Middx, UB3 3BB
Renewals: 01895 85 3740

Please return this item to the Learning Centre on
or before the last date stamped below:

808·2

WRITING HANDBOOKS

Developing Characters for Script Writing

RIB DAVIS

A & C Black • London

For Patricia, Olly and Harry

First published 2001
Reprinted 2004
A & C Black Publishers Limited
37 Soho Square, London W1D 3QZ
www.acblack.com

© 2001 Rib Davis

ISBN 0–7136–6950-0

A CIP catalogue record for this book is available
from the British Library.

A & C Black uses paper produced with elemental chlorine-free pulp,
harvested from managed sustainable forests.

Typeset in $10\frac{1}{2}$ on $12\frac{1}{2}$ pt Sabon
Printed and bound in Great Britain by
Creative Print and Design (Wales), Ebbw Vale

Contents

Acknowledgements

American Beauty Alan Ball, Newmarket Press, New York, 1999

The Birthday Party Harold Pinter, Faber and Faber, 1991

Can't Complain Rib Davis, BBC Radio play

Games for Actors and Non-Actors Augusto Boal, trans. Adrian Jackson, Routledge, 1992

Secrets and Lies Mike Leigh, Faber and Faber, 1997

Spend, Spend, Spend Jack Rosenthal, Penguin, 1978

All rights whatsoever in this play are strictly reserved and application for performance, etc., must be made before rehearsal to Casarotto Ramsay Ltd., National House, 60-66 Wardour Street, London W1V 4ND. No performance may be given unless a licence has been obtained.

Talking Heads Alan Bennett, BBC Worldwide Limited. © Alan Bennett, 1988

Taxi Driver Paul Schrader, Faber and Faber, 1990

Every effort has been made to trace and acknowledge copyright owners. If any right has been omitted the publishers offer their apologies and will rectify this in subsequent editions following notification.

Introduction

When we see a play on stage or television, or watch a film, or listen to a radio play, what is it that we remember most? It may be some stunning landscape photography, or some great dialogue, or a remarkable insight into the meaning of life. In fact, however, all these are linked through character. The insight is invariably reached through the experiences of the characters; dialogue only works if it is absolutely right for a particular character at a particular moment; landscape photography only functions fully within a film if it is saying something about the place and, ultimately, is saying something about what the people undergo in that place. Of course, we might say, 'Great photography, pity about the rest of the film,' but in that case even the photography is only succeeding in a very limited way. It all comes back to people, to characters: all the elements of a play or a film are interlinked, and the most important of those elements is character.

The first requirement of any script is that it must hold the attention of the audience through to the end. An audience that switches off or walks out is not a satisfied audience, and neither writers nor anyone else connected to a production (including funders, of course!) want a dissatisfied audience. So why does an audience stay? The principal, most basic reason is: to find out what happens next. If the audience doesn't care what happens next, then that is a crucial failing. So what makes an audience care what happens next? The answer is, above all: caring about the characters. Caring about what happens next is about caring what happens next *to the characters*. To have the audience care about the characters is, then, absolutely vital; it is central to the success of a script, whether that script is intended for television, film, stage or radio.

1

Much of what has been said above also applies to short stories and novels, where characterisation is equally important. There is one huge difference, though, between the presentation of character in, on the one hand, novels and shorts stories, and, on the other hand, the script media dealt with in this book (television, stage, film and radio). The difference is that in novels and short stories there is a voice (or, sometimes, voices) speaking directly to us, the reader. This voice, the narrator, may be in the third person or first person; it may be God-like, all-seeing and all-knowing, or it may be limited to one individual's personal experience; it may be reliable, wise and witty, or it may even not be telling the truth. But whatever else it is, a narrator is a *mediator* between the events depicted and the reader. It guides the reader through the events, very often helping us to understand characters along the way. But in the script media (with some exceptions) there is usually no such guide, no narrator to help us understand the characters and their actions. We see what they do and hear what they say, but the interpretation of character – and of the whole piece – is left to us. How to create strong, credible characters the audience will care about without recourse to a narrator is, then, one of the greatest challenges faced by the scriptwriter/playwright.

This book deals with character in all the script media. These media obviously differ from each other in a variety of respects, yet they have a great deal in common. Radio drama, for example, as it clearly cannot call upon visual effects (other than in the listener's mind), seems a very long way from film, yet in its capacity to move apparently effortlessly from location to location it closely resembles film, while television writing often seems closer to theatre than to film. The relationships between these media, then, are not always obvious, and in the coming chapters there will be many points where distinctions will be drawn between the handling of certain techniques in the various media. They do, however, have a number of major elements in common, including the need for effective dialogue, a strong plot and successful characterisation. This last is perhaps the most important of all, for it is upon characterisation that all else hinges.

Finally, a word of warning about this and every other book which presents itself as a guide to – or, worse, a manual for –

some aspect of writing. In general, I have a strong dislike of books about writing that are prescriptive, that tell you what to do and what not to do. And there are plenty of such books around. The problem is that very often the writers of these books have in mind a certain type of film (maybe the traditional Hollywood blockbuster) or a certain type of play (maybe in the naturalistic tradition), and all comments are made in the light of this. Thus one well-known book on screenwriting can blithely state that the goal of the main plot will tend to be action-based while the goal of the sub-plot will tend to be relationship-based. Well, who says? Even restricting ourselves to films, how does this apply to, say, *Citizen Kane*, or *Bonnie and Clyde*, or *Pulp Fiction* or *The Big Lebowski*? I am not entirely unsympathetic to the point: it is true that in many scripts the plot is action-based while the sub-plot is relationship-based, but despite the use of the words 'tend to' the analysis is too bald, the division too sharp, and the analysis fails sufficiently to take into account the multitude of different genres and styles in which scripts can be written. The writers of such books generally love rules (they often show some affection for diagrams, too). I don't. So what I am offering is a little advice, that is all. There are a million ways to go about writing a play or a script, and creating the characters within it. So if ever my advice slips into being prescriptive, I apologise in advance.

But then, writers don't take orders anyway.

Part 1: Notes for Creation of a Character

1. Roots of a Character

Scripts are full of characters: where do they all come from? They come from all over the place. There are no absolutes. A character might be closely based upon a particular individual known to the author, or it might (apparently, at least) be conjured out of thin air. Or it might be something between the two. It might even – as in the case with some of the characters in films by the Coën brothers – take as its starting point an actor or actress. (The character of Ed in *Raising Arizona* apparently began with the writer/director brothers wondering what sort of character it would be really fun to see Holly Hunter play.) So there are no hard and fast rules. But there are dangers.

Of family and friends

When I first started writing, I based my characters almost exclusively on family members (disguised, of course, with varying degrees of success). My family is not a particularly extended one, however, so I soon ran out of people. I moved on to friends. There were a few more of them but they, too, were rapidly exhausted. So before long I was genuinely having to create characters.

The reasons for basing my characters upon family and friends, though, were good ones: these were people I knew well. I could hear the inflections of their voices in my head, I had some knowledge of what they wanted to do with their lives, and I thought I had a pretty good idea of how they would react in the situations I was putting them in. Perhaps most importantly, I knew them in the round: I knew not only their present but much of their past, not only their obvious characteristics but also their contradictions, not only their virtues but also their weaknesses and foibles. And where I wasn't certain about particular aspects I felt that I knew so much else about them that I could convincingly fill in the gaps.

So beginning with family and friends wasn't a bad thing. They came from a world I knew – my own world – and using them as models gave me confidence, an important commodity for any writer. Actually, I felt I couldn't go wrong (even to the point of telling one director, about a character's actions, 'But this is what he actually did!' – as though that somehow guaranteed that its representation on the page was not only accurate but also undeniably appropriate for the script). Of course, I could go wrong, and did. I found myself unwittingly being loyal to the real people acting as models for these characters, on the one hand unwilling to change 'the truth' – both what these people were like and in many cases even the events that had actually happened to them – and on the other hand reluctant to dwell on their less positive attributes, although these too were 'true'. And I did not want to add or develop attributes which took them further from the originals: these, after all, were my friends! The result was often something close to blandness. By modelling my characters so firmly upon friends and family I had stunted their development, reined in the use of my imagination and constrained what ought to have been a process of organic growth within the script writing, which would have allowed the characters to develop *through the writing*. This is a theme to which I shall return.

Writing yourself

These characters, then, were closely based upon people I knew well, and their experiences were often experiences in which I had in real life been directly involved. Writing about them encouraged a tendency which needed no added encouragement – a tendency to write about myself.

We all write about ourselves, of course. Even when you think you are writing about a character or an event which has absolutely nothing to do with you personally, you look back some years later and realise – how could you ever have missed it? – that really it was all about the accident you had as a child, or coming to terms with how you had betrayed so-and-so, or dealing with the death of your closest friend. The setting may be remote and the surface details utterly different, but the need to write on this topic, to engineer that situation, to create this character, springs from deep within each of us as writers, whether we are aware of it at the time or not. And that's fine. If we don't write about what is in some way important to us, then we are unlikely to write with much conviction. But this is not to be confused with autobiographical writing, and it was autobiographical writing (masquerading as dramatic fiction, of course) that I was doing.

Basing a character upon oneself has all the advantages of using family or friends as models, but even more of the disadvantages. If we are reluctant to slur a friend (whether or not the friend recognises that he or she is being portrayed) then how much more reluctant are we to be brutally honest about ourselves? How much less willing are we to develop the character with all its complexities and negative traits?

The fact is that basing a character squarely upon oneself is severely limiting. If we limit ourselves to our own experiences and if we limit a character to what we perceive ourself to be, then we have put a straightjacket on the creative process. That is not to say that some playwrights/scriptwriters have not created wonderful characters modelled upon themselves (many of Woody Allen's leading male characters, for example, appear to be very close to Woody Allen himself) but the exercise is certainly constraining.

A reservoir of traits

But if we are not to base characters closely upon friends, family, or self, then how are they to be created at all? The answer is that we can create characters who are not based on any single individuals; rather, we can call upon that massive bank of knowledge and feelings that each of us has from the experience of having come into contact with a vast array of humanity – people we have interacted with in all sorts of ways, as well as people we haven't even met but have only heard of. All of these people's lives have somehow – directly or indirectly – come into contact with our own. The process of creating characters, then, can be seen as sewing together fragments of individuals from here, there and everywhere – not randomly, of course, but to create human beings who are both credible and right for the particular script. Perhaps more importantly, the characters can be created without our ever consciously identifying particular real people from whom we are drawing traits; rather, the traits can in effect be abstract, though, of course, they then have to be made very much flesh and blood in the form of this or that new fictional individual.

So, we don't have to take whole people or even large chunks of people. Instead, we can create characters by putting together a set of character traits, along with a setting, history, objectives and so on, secure that, when it comes to turning these traits into an active character, we will be able to call upon all our experience of human interaction to make the character live and breathe, though not necessarily resemble any one person we have ever met. It is a leap of faith, and like all such leaps it can be risky, but it can be very rewarding.

So, if we are to start to create a character from ingredients, what are the ingredients? They are in fact the very same ingredients which go to make up the personalities of each of us, the ingredients that make every one of us different from every other one of us. Very broadly speaking, they can be grouped into three categories (though they have huge areas of overlap):

1) What the character is born as/into
2) What the character acquires or becomes through experience

These two categories very roughly correspond to nature and nurture (what we inherit, and what we acquire as a result of our experiences of life). But then for script writing there is a third category:

3) What the character is now.

This third category is, in a sense, even more important than the other two, as for the most part this is what is most visible to the audience.

For any character that you are creating, the elements of each of these categories can be listed. But a confession: I am not pretending that, for every minor character – or even some major ones! – in every script that I have written, I have been through this whole process. I haven't. For some characters, certainly, there are many elements that I will not have considered at all. But whenever I have taken the trouble to be thorough in this process for any character, it has paid rich dividends.

So, the following few chapters list those elements which it is useful to consider when creating a character, along with comments. It is not a comprehensive list, but it is certainly enough to make a good start.

2. Birth Marks

We should begin by considering what the character was born as, and born into.

Gender

Is your character male or female? For some characters it may not matter too much, particularly for very minor ones, but usually gender is of major importance. We do not need to adhere to male and female stereotyping to note that men and women have widely differing attitudes *in general* on certain topics, and often *tend* to talk and act in rather different ways. The italics are important. You are not, of course, dealing with women or men in general – you are creating one woman or one man. What is important is your *awareness* of gender-differentiated values and types of behaviour, and awareness too of your audience's expectations based on these attributes. Very often, in fact, you might wish to create a character who behaves in a way that is certainly not regarded as quintessentially female or male: the character you create challenges the stereotype. There are many such examples. Thelma and Louise, in *Thelma and Louise*, for example, refuse to be as submissive as women are often expected to be, and often challenge the men they encounter. They are not, however, mere feminist ciphers: Thelma, in particular, is perfectly happy to flirt in an entirely traditional way. Similarly, while most of the male characters in the film behave in ways which conform to a fairly standard negative stereotype, that mould, too, is broken by the detective leading the hunt for them: he is in fact a sympathetic and understanding man. So gender is important, but here as in other aspects of characterisation we must beware of the cliché.

A note of warning. Writers often wish to reinforce trends of which they approve, but at the same time, of course, they must reflect society as it is. So, if we make every mechanic a woman, every senior executive a woman, every strong character a woman, the audience begins to feel the presence of a preacher. This is not society as it is but as the writer might like it to be. Better – and more convincing – is the placement of one or two key characters than the attempt utterly to distort the representation of the world, and in the process lose credibility. There is also danger on the other side: in Richard Harris' radio play *Is It Something I Said?* the one female character, Stella, is a selfish, nagging wife. She is married to one of the two central male characters, but it seems that the other man has a wife who is very similar. This is quite unpleasant gender stereotyping. The play dates from 1978, though: one would be unlikely to find such characterisation now.

If you ever doubt the importance of the decision over gender when creating your character, go and see Caryl Churchill's play *Cloud Nine*, a comedy of sexual politics (among other things) in which all the women's parts are played by men, and the men are played by women. Hearing the lines and witnessing the attitudes, seeing the movements and gestures and observing the power roles with the genders all reversed make us question gender roles and ways of looking at the world in a remarkable way. It also becomes very clear – from a writer's point of view – that changing the gender of a character really does change much more than a name. (Incidentally, Dennis Potter's wonderful television play *Blue Remembered Hills* has a comparable effect, with all the children's parts being taken by adults).

Race

Race can be absolutely central to a character's being. It can affect virtually everything about that person – upbringing, education, job prospects, social life, aspirations... everything. Just think of the Samuel L. Jackson character Zeus in *Die Hard With A Vengeance* (writer, Jonathan Hensleigh), so painfully aware of how his life choices are limited by the skin colour he was born with. And yet, very often, the race of a character does not need to be – and should not be – identified. Always stating the race of a character would not be popular with most actors, particularly those from ethnic minorities, while directors (or casting directors) like to have as free a hand as possible in selecting actors. Thankfully, long gone are the days when actors from the black or ethnic minority communities could only play particular roles specified for them (very often servants). So in general, unless there are good reasons to do otherwise, it is wise to leave the race open.

Sometimes, however, there are very good reasons to make the race specific. If either the whole piece or certain scenes are set in a neighbourhood of a particular ethnic character, or the script is in some way dealing with race or prejudice, then of course the race of each character (or certainly of each major character) has a bearing. But again, expectations and stereotypes are there to be played with. For example, Mike Leigh's *Secrets and Lies* would be rather less interesting if the main black character were not well educated while her white mother works in a cardboard box factory and her white half-sister is a road sweeper.

As before, though, a word of warning. It may seem attractive to pepper your script with characters from all varieties of ethnic backgrounds (particularly on radio, where the variety of accents can be useful at the most basic level, in identifying the speaker), but just as the audience can detect falsehood in the presentation of gender, so the handling of race has to be credible, if you are not to lose the faith of your audience.

Class

Class is hugely important, in terms of how characters are perceived and how they perceive themselves and, of course, in terms of how they are likely to speak and act. Naturally, when making a note about a character's class, the basic categories that we use – lower, middle and upper – may well be extremely crude. When these categories are used, is class being defined through income, lifestyle, occupation, parents' class, or a combination of all the above, and if so in what proportions? The sub-categories – upper-middle, for example, or aristocratic, or 'underclass' – are not much of an improvement, as they too fail to recognise the complexity of identifying features. Neverthe-less, in creating a character, when in our notes we place a charac-ter in a particular class we do make a statement about that character, even if the statement has to be immediately qualified.

Class has become increasingly hard to identify. A labourer on an oil rig may earn more than a university lecturer; many of the unemployed are graduates. In Britain, dividing lines have become blurred, partly because of the decline of large-scale manufacturing industry and its associated 'class loyalty' and at the same time the eagerness of many to ascribe to themselves the identity of 'middle-class'. Class mobility has increased; it is not at all uncommon for someone describing themself as middle-class also to state that their parents are working-class. So while a particular class is something we are born into, it is also something we may move away from, either in fact or at least in our own perceptions. And this is one of the most fertile areas for the creator of character – the identity which we ascribe to ourself, which may not be the same identity others ascribe to us. This discrepancy may manifest itself in all sorts of ways: a character may look in the mirror and see a natural leader, while others see only a hesitant lieutenant; a character such as Polonius in *Hamlet* may believe himself to be plain-speaking and concise – 'since brevity is the soul of wit' – while everyone else knows him to be an insufferable windbag. This type of discrepancy between perceptions is particularly potent in the area of class: there is the upper-class character who is determined to be 'of the people' but succeeds only in being patronising, or, to refer to Mike Leigh's work once more, there is Beverly in *Abigail's Party*, determined to be (the worst sort of) middle-class but with (the worst sort of) working-class tastes and attitudes all entirely apparent. (This uneasy border between working- and middle-class, with its associated aspirations and pretentiousness, is also a recurring theme in the work of Willy Russell, from *Breezeblock Park* to *Educating Rita*.)

It is important, then, to have a clear idea of your character's class, clear not in a simplified way but rather recognising the possible ambiguities, contradictions and complexities – and maybe guilt, or pride – associated with the class position of your character.

Family background

It is not necessary to be a psychoanalyst to recognise that much of what any character becomes is as a result of that character's family background and family relationships. First of all, what sort of a family is it? – not just in terms of class, but in terms of its particular characteristics. Is it, for example, an artistic family, or an intellectual one, a warm family of a cold one, or a non-communicative one? Any of these may or may not apply to any family of any class.

Then when considering a specific character, there are such basic elements as position in the family: only child? eldest child? middle? youngest? Of course, what we become is not crudely dictated by such matters, but they do have an effect. Being youngest might lead to being spoilt, or dominated, or neglected, for example.

But perhaps you – the scriptwriter – are already becoming impatient. Why bother with all of this, you may ask. What does it matter how the character has become what he or she is? – what matters is what the character is now. This is true to some extent. Despite having mapped out the family relationships of a character, when it comes to the script itself there may not be a single reference to any family relationships. But this is not the point. The point is that *you* should know exactly where this character is coming from, and that knowledge informs your creation of the character in the round. The script may not refer to what made the character what she or he is, but you need to know this in order to make the character what she or he is. The more you know about the character, the more confident and secure you will feel in the writing, the more rounded the character will be. Furthermore, when we ask the questions – what is this character's relationship with mother, father, brother(s), sister(s), grandparent(s), step- and half-siblings, etc. – then *the very act of posing these questions acts as stimulation to developing new aspects of the character*, in turn leading to new possibilities for the narrative, new elements of the plot. For characterisation is not merely a matter of filling in details of a character, with a plot already decided. Rather, the two should develop if possible *organically*, together. But more of this later.

Name

When the names of real people are chosen by their parents there are often deliberations which go on for months – in fact it is far from unknown for a child still not to have a fixed name for weeks after coming into the world. Names are important. While, of course, anyone might be called John or Paul or Jane or Sarah, there are very few upper-class British women named Tracy, or white men named Mustapha, or working-class children called Sebastian, or Britons of the twenty-first century named Charity or Obadiah.

Names, then, often betray class and race as well as period; the writer may choose to do more than this. In the seventeenth century Jonson would use names like Subtle, Doll, Lovewit, Common or Mammon. The essential characteristic of each individual was made perfectly clear. In more modern times writers have tended to use names with less obvious meanings, but still in Willy Loman (in Miller's *Death of a Salesman*) it is hard to avoid the meaning of 'low man', while the un-stated irony of his son being called Happy is that he isn't, and then in another play of Miller's, *The Price*, we have Solomon, who, of course, appears to be wise. Then in the film *Cast Away* the protagonist is named Chuck Noland, whose name also appears to foretell his destiny. In general, however, characters' names in scripts nowadays are not likely to carry symbolism, and if we try too hard to inject them with it we run the risk of showing the author's hand too openly (though this does, of course, depend on the genre: the more stylised the genre, the less the audience is likely to object to an openly symbolic name).

One last note on names: don't feel that the name of a character is the first thing that has to be established about him or her. Just as very often when I have written a script the title has been the last element to have been decided upon (titles often come from within the script itself), so when creating a character you might well find it useful to come to a number of other decisions before deciding upon a name, and even then (again as with the script) the name may only be a 'working name' (as in 'working title') – don't be afraid to change it at any stage in the planning or writing process. (But if you change it when much of the script has been written, do try if possible to change it for a name of the same number of syllables, as otherwise this is likely to upset the rhythm of many of the sentences in which the name is used.) It may seem superficial to say so, but sometimes changing a name really can help you to see a character in a completely new way! Such is the power of labels.

3. Learning through Experience

We now move on to what the character acquires or becomes through experience.

Education

Education is, of course, closely linked to both class and occupation. Education will have had a huge impact on the life of your character, both academically and socially. So whether or not it is ever directly mentioned in the script, you should always have a clear idea of how the character has been educated. Was it at private school, comprehensive, secondary modern, grammar? If at private school, was it boarding or not? What sort of results did the character attain? Who did he or she mix with? Did he or she go on to college or university, or study later in life?

As with other elements of characterisation, *it is not merely the facts of the matter that are important but also – probably more so – the attitudes surrounding the facts*. Many of us are proud of our education, but for widely differing reasons. Those who have been to Oxford or Cambridge, for example, invariably find some pretext to mention the fact upon your first meeting them: where others would say 'when I was at university' these people will usually say 'when I was at Oxford' or 'at Cambridge'. Clearly there is some pride in having attended these institutions, but there is also an element of displaying the badge, raising status by making clear the supposed superiority of education received. Your character may be like this or, perhaps more interestingly, may be one of the minority who detest such institutions despite having gone there. Either way it is the attitude that is the important thing, the most revealing aspect so far as characterisation is concerned. Similarly one may be proud of having attended the local comprehensive, or may resent it. Again it is the relationship with the education as much as the education itself that is of interest to the writer.

Abilities

Many of these categories are obviously very closely linked. This category of abilities is clearly linked to education and also to passions, but still abilities need to be noted separately. A character might play the piano, for example, but be really passionate about fishing (or, for that matter, be a fisherman with a real passion for playing the piano). And abilities are not always directly connected to education. As a mature adult the character might become a good sailor, without ever having sailed earlier in life.

Very often we think of individuals as being 'intelligent' or 'able', and while such generalised statements (negative as well as positive) are of some use when making notes to create a character, it is more helpful to be much more specific. For example, I know both a brilliant university lecturer in the arts who is at the same totally unable to fathom simple percentages, and also an excellent car mechanic who can hardly read.

So, for a character note, rather than state 'highly intelligent' you might want to note, say, 'perceptive at reading the stock market'. Certainly many highly intelligent people are not perceptive at reading the stock market. Even better might be, 'perceptive at reading the stock market, but often fails to act on her readings.' Here we have more than just an ability – we have the use to which the ability is put, or not. And we have the ability leading us on to another character trait, though so far it is not clear precisely what this trait is. Is this character generally timid? Or does she have no spare money at all to risk on the market? Or does she see the stock market only as a game? Whatever the explanation, here we have a character note that indicates an ability and also hints at much more about the character; the results in a script would probably leave the audience wanting to know the answers, and that is the condition we always want our audience to be in.

As in other areas, try to avoid always allotting the most pre-dictable abilities. Sometimes it is quite right to show the aristo-crat having the ability to play polo rather well, as we might expect, or the middle-aged lorry-driver from Barnsley being able to train pigeons, but it might be interesting to have the aristocrat be an excellent mathematician, while the lorry-driver is a medium who is able to levitate. Neither of these skills may be used a great deal (the lorry driver may even be terrified by his own abilities) but each of them could turn a standard character into a memorable one. This is not to say that every character has to have an unusual ability in order to be memorable – there are many attributes that can make a character memorable – but rather that it is one of many options.

Own family

'Own family' here means the family that the character has a part in creating, rather than the family he or she is born into. So it refers to husband/wife/partner, children and in-laws, and the relationships between this character and those other members of the family.

Drama is to a very large extent driven through conflict, and through attempts at resolving conflict, either through some form of compromise or some form of victory/defeat. As we all know, families are very often seething with conflicts. And as we always remain within families (in many instances even divorce does not end the family relationship) there is a claustrophobic element in conflicts within the family. Family relationships matter: we are very rarely able simply to walk away from them. So if as a writer you choose to depict a conflict about, say, land, or business ethics, or over sexual jealousy – whatever – you always have the option of placing that conflict between two unrelated individuals or between two members of the same family. Placing the relationship within the family 'ups the ante', as whatever happens as a result of the conflict will then affect all sorts of other relation-ships within the family, and all sorts of pressures from within the family will probably be brought to bear to try to solve the conflict one way or another, either to maintain the stability and unity of the family or, alternatively, to consolidate new power bases within the family.

Passions run high in families, so any conflict that would anyway produce strong emotional responses from characters can be raised to new levels if placed within the family. *Hamlet* is not merely about the usurpation of a throne, it is about the murder of a father and betrayal by a wife; *Death of a Salesman* is not merely about the failure of a man on the road, it is about a man's inability to tell the truth to his wife and children, and their resulting inability to be truthful back to him. Not all great dramas are set within families, but certainly a family setting can raise the stakes, raise the tensions, and raise the resonance of the whole piece.

I make the distinction here between family – what a character is born into – and 'own family' – the family a character creates, partly to emphasise the element of choice. As noted earlier, all our lives are a combination of what we are born into – over which we have no choice – and what we choose. So we may resent our parents or siblings, but we know that we have not chosen them and thus ultimately are not responsible for them. Of course, we may still be ashamed of the family we are born into, or proud of it, or frustrated by the very fact of never being able to escape it, but most of us do not take personal responsibility for having been born into our own families. We are responsible, on the other hand, for the choices we make, and these include the partners that we select, the decision to have children and the manner of their upbringing. This is an important distinction that can be explored in the creation of a character, as choices can bring with them regrets. A character may regret the choice of spouse, regret having children, regret how they have brought the children up, and there is a responsibility here for these relationships which is greater than in the birth family relationships. That is not to say that conflicts arising out of one's 'own' family are of any greater or lesser intensity than those arising out of one's 'birth' family, but they may have the different colouring of this particular type of responsibility. (This is obviously a matter of perspective, however, depending upon which character we are focusing upon; one character's own family relationship will be another character's birth family relationship.)

As in every other aspect of planning a character, it is not the mere facts that are important but the character's attitude to the facts; it is not the fact that the character has his or her own family but rather the nature of the relationships which needs to be established, and the attitude of the character towards being – to a considerable extent at least – responsible for what those relationships are.

Sexuality

At its simplest, this is merely a matter of whether or not the character is heterosexual. Of course, usually this does not need to be specified in the script itself, though on other occasions it is central to a character. For example, the fact that Carter Heywood in the television comedy series *Spin City* is gay is not merely incidental: it is one of his major defining features and also supplies the opportunity for a stream of gay/straight jokes. Or there is George, the gay character in *My Best Friend's Wedding* (writer, Ronald Bass). Here, the fact that he is gay simplifies matters: we know that there is no possibility of his fake amorous relationship with the Julia Roberts character becoming a reality. These, then, are examples of gay characters where the sexual orientation of the character is central to the character's purpose within the script.

But there are also gay characters in scripts (particularly over recent years) for no particular reason: they are not gay because this will allow such-and-such to take place, but rather they are gay simply because many people are, so why should this character not be? Sometimes, it should be noted, this comes about as a matter of casting rather than anything being specified in the script, and thus is analogous to parts being taken by black actors without any specification – with the difference, of course, that it is very often not apparent whether an actor is gay or not.

I recently wrote a script, *What Was Coming To Him*, for a youth theatre in which one of the male performers was very openly and obviously gay. This acted as the spur to creating the character of God as a gay man; the fact of his being gay, although obvious through every gesture of the actor, was never directly referred to in the script and did not directly affect the plot, but it did fit well with the creation of a God who in other respects was also far from the standard image of the Almighty. So while God here was gay simply because he could be (and why shouldn't he be?) the casting also raised the question of whether it had ever been declared that God must be heterosexual, and, if such a declaration had been made, why?

But sexuality is not only about sexual orientation, it is about sexual attitudes. These are of great importance, as they obviously affect a character's choice of partners and sex life, and at the same time sexual attitudes are very much bound up with the character's morality. Is this character a sexual predator, say, or sexually submissive? How strong is this character's sexual appetite, and does he or she always give in to it? (In one memorable exchange in an episode of *Frasier*, in the course of a conversation about refusing sex Niles remarks to Ros that of course she knows what sort of reaction you get when you say 'No' to your partner, but Ros only manages to stutter a feeble agreement – it becomes clear that she has in fact never said 'No' to a man!)

Attitudes towards sex and sexuality have of course changed enormously over recent decades. In very broad terms, in the 1960s and 1970s there was a new openness about sex and sexuality, which was then followed by the rise of the women's movement (although, of course, the roots of that existed much earlier) – felt right through society – which in turn appears to have given rise to the more recent laddish culture. So, the sexual attitudes of your character will in part be a result of his or her age. During our formative years we tend to take on the attitudes of the culture around us, and we do not always change these attitudes with the changing times. This is not to say, of course, that everyone of any given age will have the same attitudes towards sex and sexuality – of course they won't – but rather there will be a tendency to see things in a particular way. So a woman now who was twenty in, say, the late 1970s, might well be shocked by her own daughter's lack of political sexual awareness today. If our characters of all ages are to be credible, then we must take great care to take account of how attitudes have (in general) changed from generation to generation, and this particularly applies to attitudes towards sex and sexuality.

Back-story

Back-story is the story of what has happened to the character up to the point where we join him or her, that is, it is the story before the 'now' presented in the script. There is some ambiguity here, though, for sometimes a back-story is actually shown as part of the action, most commonly through someone remembering. If enough of the back-story is shown, it can become the story itself. In Miller's *Death of a Salesman*, for example, what we see from the past of the Loman family is not merely remembered – rather, it is being *lived* at that moment in the head of Willy.

Back-story is, in a sense, a part of characterisation, in that it is a series of events which you note, and decide to refer to (or sometimes show) or not in the script itself. In another sense, though, back-story has more to do with plot. It is essentially about what has *happened*. The major decision connected with it is really where to place the *now* in relation to these events. Let us say, for example, that our script is dealing with an adult woman who was psychologically abused as a teenager. We can find out about this event as the script progresses, but as the woman concerned shows herself in other ways to be untrustworthy, we as audience doubt whether the abuse ever really took place. And it may be, for example, that convincing the audience that this really did happen, and then bringing the abuser to book, is a major element of the plot of the script. The psychological abuse, then, is a major element of the back-story. But the same events could be handled very differently. Our telling of the story could start with the abuse itself. This then becomes the first event in the plot, and is no longer back-story at all. This immediately removes any doubts we might have had about the events taking place, and as a result the script will need a new focus. And the abuse would no longer be something to note under 'character's back-story' but would be part of the script.

In planning your script, be flexible about this. You may begin by thinking that an event should be shown as part of the main sequence of events, but then realise that there is more to be gained by turning it into back-story, or vice-versa.

Remember: the plot, the back-story, the characters – they are all your invention; never be tied to your original plans for the sake of it; change whatever you need to change as you go along to make the piece work as well as it can. Think of your script as an organism rather than a mechanism.

4. The Character Now

Age

When it comes actually to writing the script, many of the characteristics about which you may have made notes will not appear in the script at all. But the age of all but the most minor characters must be stated. This is because the age of any character is of crucial importance. In their middle age or even old age many people profess to feeling or even acting just as they did in their younger days, but this is not the point. Whether we like it or not, age affects all of a character's relationships, and, as noted immediately above, the period of that character's formative years will have been central to the establishing of the character's attitudes. As with other attributes, though, we can have fun by writing against expectation: the little old lady may take a tremendous interest in sex; the teenage lad may be seriously concerned about the morals of the country having gone to the dogs.

Occupation

When asked to talk about ourselves, many of us begin by saying what it is we do for a living. Occupation is seen as a major element (perhaps *the* major element) in our definition of self and of each other. So occupations for characters should be chosen with care. Sometimes, of course, a character's working life is of major importance to the plot (clearly spy dramas have to have spies) but on other occasions there will be more apparent freedom. We want to choose the occupation for the character that reflects that character's personality and position in the world, and also casts light upon other aspects of the script. We make certain assumptions about, say, a house painter, or a senior business executive. A particular occupation not only carries with it a particular status but also implies certain levels of education, class and, perhaps, ambition. These are all assumptions that the writer can play with. So the senior business executive might in fact be working class, never having gone to university, while the house painter might have a strangely educated accent. For what is most important here is not the work itself but rather how the characters relate to their jobs. Are they satisfied, bored, bitter, excited by their work? Have they tried to stand aside from the competitive world, or have they tried but given up on attempting to climb any higher up the greasy pole? Or are they still determined to get to the top by any possible means? What satisfaction do they get from their work, or does it pay the bills and nothing more? So it is this *relationship* between the character and the job that is of interest to the writer (and the audience).

In allocating an occupation to your character, also ask yourself: is this what the character *ought* to be doing? As occupations offer varying degrees of not only financial reward but also social standing to their holders, ask yourself: is there a discrepancy between, on the one hand, the job you have allocated to this character, and, on the other, the job that this character would be capable of. If there is a discrepancy, that does not necessarily mean that you should change the job of the character; rather, it may well offer an opportunity to explore the mis-match: is the character aware of the discrepancy, and, if so, what is the character's attitude towards it? As with every element of characterisation, here again it is not so much the facts that matter but the characters' attitudes towards the facts. In some scripts, such as *Wall Street* (the world of high finance) or *The Full Monty* (the world of the unemployed) or Shaw's *Mrs Warren's Profession* (the world of prostitution) an occupation is at the centre of the characterisation, but in each case it is the attitudes of the characters towards their occupations and – crucially – the question of whether their position in society is deserved that holds our attention.

Let us explore the character and occupation of William Thacker (Hugh Grant) in the film *Notting Hill*. His shop is the setting in which the two main characters can meet. But that is not the main point – there are many settings in which they could have been made to meet. Why might the writer (Richard Curtis) have chosen to make William the owner of a less than hugely successful travel bookshop? What does it say about him, and what are its implications for the rest of the script?

The fact that William owns a bookshop at all implies a certain intellectualism, which places his world (and that of his friends) a very long way away from that of the glamorous film star character Anna Scott. And it is specifically a travel bookshop, which places him even further from the general commercialism associated with an ordinary bookshop, though on the other hand it is not concerned with the purely intellectual as, say, a university bookshop would be. There is nothing pretentious, flashy or even mildly ambitious about this bookshop; it is modest and unassuming, like the character who runs it. But even some travel bookshops might conceivably be successful; this bookshop very clearly is not, but William still wishes to stick with it, implying that for him what is worthwhile is not a matter of money. This is important: it is one thing to have the hugely rich film star enter into a relationship with a poor man (which might lead him to be dazzled by dollar signs) but it is quite another to have the relationship with a poor man *for whom money is not important*. This is further emphasised by his friends, who celebrate the quality of a restaurant established by one of their number even though it has failed to survive: the spirit of the attempt is what matters to them. But self-righteousness is avoided, partly by self-deprecating humour, and partly by the fact that another in the group is equally unsuccessful in the more commercial world of the City. So the choice of unsuccessful travel bookshop owner says a great deal about this character, and fits perfectly with the other elements of the script.

Sometimes the occupation of a character will not only reflect that character but will also be of symbolic significance. For example, Halder, the character drawn further and further into the Nazi extermination machine in C.P. Taylor's *Good*, is, of all things, a doctor. Or there is Solomon (we have already commented upon the name) in Arthur Miller's *The Price* who, in a play which weighs up the value of people's lives, has the job of 'registered appraiser'. Or there is the character in Dario Fo's political farce *Accidental Death of an Anarchist*, named Maniac, whose 'twenty years of intensive training in sixteen different loony bins under some of the best shrinks in the biz' appears to make 'maniac' his occupation. The occupation here clearly carries an ironic symbolism, as in his madness he is also one of the few sources of sanity in the play (as could be said of the Fool in a number of Shakespeare's plays).

At a more mundane level, in choosing an occupation, we should keep an eye out for the less obvious businesses. We shouldn't forget the cable drum wholesalers, the barge-repairers, the pyrotechnic engineers or those who make a living selling re-manufactured inkjet cartridges for computer printers. The world is a hugely varied place and, quite apart from anything else, it is so much fun to show some of that variety. At the same time you can be giving your characters special micro-worlds all of their own, helping to make them not only distinctive but also memorable.

This is as good a place as any to mention the place of research in the creation of character. Character creation should not be rushed, and if there is a world of a particular character (or, as is very often the case, a particular character's occupation) which you don't know enough about – find out before you put fingers to keyboard. I once spent the best part of three years researching prison life, reading everything I could get my hands on, as well as interviewing prison officers and ex-inmates. In the resulting two scripts (one for stage, the other for radio) I only used a tiny fraction of what I had learned, but they were two of the best scripts I have ever written.

Thorough research pays off.

However, there are some things which are at least to some extent beyond research, and these are mainly to do with class, regional variation and race. It is very difficult to research speech patterns with which one does not normally come into contact. Thus, in my case, I could not envisage having as a central character a Jamaican, say. I even have difficulty sustaining convincing dialogue for upper-class characters. Information can be researched (and if in doubt about how to approach it, you might like to consult *Research for Writers*, by Ann Hoffmann), but speech patterns are very hard to imitate unless you have been exposed to them quite consistently. So my advice is not to attempt to create a major character whose speech patterns are unfamiliar. For everything else, though: do the research.

Friends and enemies

It is often said that each of us may be known by looking at our friends. So in creating a character we also create other characters: we create characters with whom this character would choose to spend time, and we also create characters whom this character would attempt to avoid. So characterisation has an infectious quality: in making one we start to make another.

In *The Big Lebowski*, for example, the Dude's choice of friends, Donny and Walter, says a lot about the Dude himself. Walter may have his moments of uncontrolled aggression and Donny may at times be somewhat simple, but while all three characters are entirely distinct the two friends are both essentially as good-hearted as the Dude himself. Sometimes, though, things are more complicated. In *The Opposite of Sex* (writer, Don Roos), for example, the morality of the major characters is not clear-cut, and friendships similarly are not entirely fixed: the central character is in many ways confused, and this is reflected in who she chooses to see as friends and enemies, fluctuating through the script. Again it is the nature of the allegiances which tells us a great deal about the character, and also about the emotional journey of the character.

Appearance

What does the character look like? In our everyday lives most of us take some care over our appearance, knowing that it makes a particular impression. First there is the body: do we make the effort to stay in shape? Do we care if we have a paunch? Do we decide that our hair is to be worn long or short, and why? And then there are the clothes. If we want to be taken seriously, we dress in a way that tries to make this clear; if we feel like flirting, we might dress to imply that, too.

Or we might want both – to be taken seriously and at the same time to indicate that we don't mind being flirtatious (the Greta Scacchi character in *Presumed Innocent* is dressed in just such a way). Even the character who pays no attention to clothes is making a (possibly unintentional) statement about his or her character, perhaps wanting to appear spontaneous, natural, untamed or anti-establishment.

As appearance matters to us in 'real life', so similarly it must matter to the scriptwriter, the creator of character. Obviously appearance is a more superficial matter than belief, but nevertheless in extreme cases an individual's appearance may be a major element – even in real life – in the formation of that character. For example, someone who has a birthmark across the face is unlikely to be psychologically unaffected by it, just as a woman of stunning beauty (or man, but in our society it is more likely to be clear in the case of a woman) is also likely to have been psychologically affected by her physical appearance.

Now, for an example of physical appearance in script writing, let's look at the opening lines in the script of *Taxi Driver*, written by Paul Schrader:

> TRAVIS BICKLE, *aged twenty-six, lean, hard, the consummate loner. On the surface he appears good-looking, even handsome; he has a quiet steady look and a disarming smile which flashes from nowhere, lighting up his whole face. But behind that smile, around his dark eyes, in his gaunt cheeks, one can see the ominous strains caused by a life of private fear, emptiness and loneliness. He seems to have wandered in from a land where it is always cold, a country where the inhabitants seldom speak. The head moves, the expression changes, but the eyes remain ever-fixed, unblinking, piercing empty space.*
> TRAVIS *is now drifting in and out of the New York City night life, a dark shadow among darker shadows. Not noticed, with no reason to be afraid,* TRAVIS *is one with his surroundings. He wears rider jeans, cowboy boots, a plaid western shirt and a worn beige Army jacket with a patch reading 'King Kong Company, 1968–70'.*
> *He has the smell of sex about him: sick sex, repressed sex,*

lonely sex, but sex none the less. He is a raw male force, driving forward; towards what, one cannot tell. Then one looks closer and sees the inevitable. The clock spring cannot be wound continually tighter. As the earth moves towards the sun TRAVIS BICKLE *moves towards violence.*

First, it should be admitted that this is somewhat unusual, both in the length of character description given and the lyrical style. This is a script, after all, not a novel, and most such stage directions (strictly speaking, this extract is a stage direction) restrict themselves to the straightforwardly factual. We should remember that everything provided in a stage direction is for the benefit of the actor playing the part (here, Robert de Niro), the director and the rest of the cast and crew – but not, directly, the audience. The audience watching a film or play doesn't read the words of stage direction (though they may, of course, if they buy the script).

So, what does this stage direction provide? It provides physical detail about this man's face and body, so we are told about the leanness, the gaunt cheeks. But also – and much more important – we are told how his physical appearance reflects his character: we are invited to see behind the smile to the fear and loneliness. Then we are told about his clothes, a combination of cowboy and fake military. Here too the details are not important in themselves but in what they might imply about this character – an urban man with a hint of fantasy about him, apparently relaxed and yet with aggression. Finally, we are given the short paragraph which is purely about this man's sexuality and wound-up aggression, something which it seems we can see in him – or, as the writer puts it, we can smell.

All of this is tremendously useful to all those involved with the production, particularly the actor playing the part, trying to get a feel for the character. If you watch *Taxi Driver* you will see that the physical description tallies very closely.

Whether the psychological description is kept to as faithfully it is more difficult to say. It seems to me that de Niro brings also a strange and compelling sort of innocence to the part, absent from this initial description. But as a writer, in giving your stage directions you are really only giving starting points for the actor and director. It is a great mistake to try to control every last piece of physical (not to mention psychological) detail through stage directions. The piece must be allowed to grow, through the input of actors, director, and those providing costume, lighting, sound and the rest. In fact if we were to continue reading the script of *Taxi Driver* and compare it with the finished film we would find that the opening sequence of visuals (which come immediately after that which is quoted above) is actually quite different from that laid down in the script. But the sequence is different in detail, not in spirit, and that is what is important. Similarly, even the specifics of physical appearance prescribed in a script may not be followed in a production. The details provided by the writer have served their purpose in pointing the actor, director and others in the direction of the characterisation, but those working on the production may then find other – and sometimes even better – ways of presenting this characterisation. Of course, there may be some details which you might absolutely insist on keeping but, in general, when it comes to physical appearance it is wise not to be too inflexible. The physical appearance denotes the interior, and so long as that interior is still suggested, the details themselves are of only secondary importance.

View of the world

We all have a view of the world, a way of looking at life. Each of your central characters needs a clear view of the world. As we will see in the analysis of the film *When Harry Met Sally*, the two protagonists there have just such clear views of existence: Sally is positive, optimistic, imperturbable, believing that everything will be fine, while Harry has a deep dread of the future, a tendency to analyse events and possible future events in such a way as always to see a negative outcome.

A view of the world does not always have to be stated, or at least does not have to be stated *as a view of the world*. That that is what it is, is up to the audience to conclude. Sometimes one character may comment *to another* (when there is sufficient reason to do so, but not otherwise) that that other person has a way of looking at the world, but this information should never feel as if it has been planted in the dialogue to inform the reader. So when Harry finally explodes to Sally that 'Nothing gets to you!' he is uttering something that we have long been aware of, so it is not said for our benefit; rather, at this point *he needs* to say it. I stress this point because sometimes, in scripts from less experienced writers, such is the anxiety to differentiate between characters, that the writer has the characters virtually describe themselves to the audience, for no particularly good reason in terms of the drama. This is generally to be avoided. (Though there are exceptions to even this. Sometimes having a character *narrate* to the audience about their own way of looking at the world can be very effective. This may be, for example, because what we are hearing is contradicted by what we are seeing at the same moment, or it may be because the particular world view is controversial, or is not accepted – the writer may hope – by most of the audience: the thief explaining that theft is not really immoral but is perfectly normal; the hang-'em and flog-'em merchant telling us why corporal and capital punishment is what this society needs. It is when patent self-description of a world view is forcibly stuffed into *dialogue* that we need to be really careful.)

Beliefs

Most of us rarely speak about our beliefs. Of course, evangelists of all varieties – Protestant, Communist, Conservative, Vegetarian or whatever – tell all the world how they ought to be living, but most of us wear our beliefs more lightly. That does not mean, however, that we do not have them. We all live by our own personal set of beliefs, whether or not we acknowledge the fact to ourselves, but in the normal way not only do we not state those beliefs, but we are not pressed even to come to any conclusions as to what they are. But drama is not 'in the normal way'.

Drama is at its best when it forces characters (and therefore the audience) first to explore their own beliefs and then to test them. This may necessitate discovering for the first time what those beliefs are. In the film *A Civil Action* (writer, Steven Zillian), for example, we have a lawyer (played by John Travolta) who in his business decisions is motivated almost entirely by money. He is not a bad or immoral man, but he is not willing to take any risks where money is involved. So when he takes on a water pollution case which he had previously refused to touch it is because he stumbles upon the fact that the potential defendant is a hugely rich company, well able to make his efforts worthwhile. But it is only as the case progresses – and he takes more and more risks, ultimately losing all his possessions – that he comes to realise there are other things worth working and fighting for. The situation he is placed in forces him to examine his own beliefs. But it is not as simple as this, for he does not simply become good-heartedly altruistic – there are other elements mixed in as well. While everyone is telling him that the sensible thing to do would be to reach an out-of-court settlement, part of his motivation in seeing the case through appears to be sheer bloody-mindedness, along with professional pride. Certainly it becomes hugely important to him to gain an apology for those who have suffered through the poisoning of the water, but an ambiguity persists – even to the end we are still left trying to work out his precise motivation.

And this is a good thing. A character should be both *credible* and *intriguing*, and this balance is not always easy to achieve. Of course the simplest characters are credible – they are driven by one straightforward, over-riding belief, but unless that belief is challenged, and they begin to doubt their belief, such a character is rarely of great interest. On the other hand it is easy to create a character who is intriguing, a character we do not fully understand, but if motivation is left too indeterminate then that character's actions may cease to be credible, or we may become impatient with the whole production.

One example of this may be Terence Davies' film *The House of Mirth* (from the novel by Edith Wharton). Here there is a romance that is never allowed to bloom fully between the two central characters, Lilly and Selden. They appear to love each other, and they certainly try to care for each other, but they never commit themselves. In an interview about the film Terence Davies makes clear that this relationship never comes to fruition – in this case, marriage – because as a result of her class and upbringing at that time the woman could not contemplate marrying a man without money and the man would never put her in that position. This makes sense, and once we have been told this we see that it is entirely consistent with what we might gather from watching the film, but unfortunately it never becomes sufficiently clear in the film itself. Certainly there is a fascination in trying to unravel the ambiguities around her wanting him and yet at the same time rejecting him, but this audience, at least, felt dissatisfied. The characterisation was intriguing but the motivation was just too ambiguous for the film to fulfil its potential. Until I saw the interview with the director, I couldn't understand why people were doing what they were doing, and thus while watching the film I ultimately felt doubts about the credibility of the characters – despite enjoying it immensely in almost every other way!

I am, of course, not calling for excuses to be found for characters to give voice to their beliefs and motivations – nothing could be more tedious – but if we are left too far in doubt then the results can be slightly disappointing.

In some cases, such as *A Civil Action*, then, characters actually find out what they believe. In other cases we can create a script where their most basic beliefs are challenged. For example, virtually everyone believes that eating people is wrong, but what of plane crash survivors in the mountains who must eat the dead or die themselves (*Alive*)? Or, we know that killing people is wrong, but what of putting out of misery someone enduring a slow and painful death, or what of suicide in such circumstances (*Whose Life Is It Anyway?*)? In each of these a basic belief is challenged. But, to be honest, such issue-based pieces have a tendency to explore the issues themselves rather than the characters involved in them, since the beliefs themselves are so generally held as to say little about the particular characters involved. Clearly how each character responds to such a situation does open avenues for more interesting differentiation between individuals, but the results in such scripts can be somewhat crude. More subtle examinations of belief are likely to be more arresting.

General manner

The general manner of a character is always very much tied up with other elements, particularly sense of humour, tension level, use of language and, of course, view of the world, but even putting all these aside for the moment it is possible to refer to a general manner. Is this character generally serious or light-hearted, a close observer of events or utterly inattentive, off-hand or officious, bumbling or efficient? Is this character generally warm or cold? A careful considerer of the facts or whimsically capricious? Arrogant or humble? Of course you don't need to answer all these questions – and there may be others you do wish to answer – but at least going over them in your mind may help you to establish the kind of person you are creating. And while each of these descriptive words is hugely general, it can nevertheless be of some assistance, even if (or particularly if) it leads you to decide that a character at first appears to be humble but is in fact arrogant, or has an efficient manner which disguises a bumbling-through, or has a manner which is serious and light-hearted by turns. Generalisations are only generalisations, but they are not without their uses.

Particular mannerisms (and even the general manner) of a character will often be influenced by the actor playing that character, but the writer may nevertheless have a major input (as Schrader does in the *Taxi Driver* extract above). Some physical mannerisms may be extremely revealing. In Alan Bleasdale's brilliant series of television plays entitled *GBH*, for example, as the central character succumbs further and further to the effects of stress, a mannerism that begins as merely a frequent emphasising of points by a gesture of the hand becomes a movement of the arm and eventually a frequent involuntary violent flailing of both arm and hand into the air. This is a man who has lost control, a man whose impulse to control all around him has itself spun out of control, and the mannerism demonstrates this.

Sense of humour

What sort of a sense of humour does this character have? Here we are dealing with two elements: firstly, what the character may say and do that is amusing (or which he or she believes might be amusing), and, secondly, the character's appreciation of humour.

There are some people who seem to have no interest in humour at all. They are a real rarity. Of more interest is the character with apparently no sense of humour who is then suddenly and inexplicably sent into paroxysms by some inoffensive remark. We are at least left asking ourselves why, even if we have no answer. But such characters are highly unusual. More commonly, there are characters who are genuinely witty, with a sharpness of mind reflected in a speed of tongue. Such wit may be sophisticated and challenging, responding moment by moment to the fabric of the conversation. Then there are others who are equally rapid in their thought but travel on cruder rails, continually using *double-entendres*, perhaps with a predictability that is ultimately tedious. Others again may not be witty in this sense at all, but may have a store of amusing (possibly true) anecdotes. And finally there are those whose primary source of humour is the packaged joke. The best of such joke-tellers are very amusing indeed, while the worst are, of course, truly wearying.

So, what sort of humour does your character employ? It may be a mixture of all these, but which predominates? And then, does this character's humour have a general aim? Is it generally used merely to lighten the conversation, or is it often employed subtly to undermine or deflate others? Is it used as a tool of aggression? Or, on the other hand, your character may habitually use humour (very often, but not exclusively, joke-telling) as a means of avoiding real engagement with others; he or she may use it to conceal feelings or vulnerabilities that otherwise might become apparent – this character is using humour as a shield.

As with other elements of characterisation, we should be aware that most individuals use a mixture of types of humour for a mixture of purposes, but it is still helpful to ask oneself about general tendencies within a character.

We then come on to appreciation of humour. It may be that there is nothing to be said about your character on this point; he or she is receptive to most types of humour. It may be, on the other hand, that your character laughs at almost everything (in an attempt to ingratiate?), or perhaps chooses only to appreciate the humour of certain other individuals (people of high

status?), thus using appreciation of humour as a means of con-
ferring favour upon some and not others, and showing which
group they wish to be seen as part of. Receiving humour, then,
just as much as producing it, can be a reflection of character.

Tension levels

Actors talk about tension levels. They will refer to a particular
character in a particular scene being at a particular level of
tension, usually calibrated from level 1 to level 7. Level 1 would
be complete relaxation, almost at the point of restful sleep,
while one might be at level 7 when holding a baby in a stuck lift
just having heard an announcement that a bomb is about to go
off in the building. And there are all the levels in between. Actors
normally use these levels to help them approach a particular
scene, or a particular moment in a scene, but they can also be
used by the writer as a way of thinking about a character in
general. Some characters are *in general* more tense than others.
The character of Simon, Daphne's least-liked brother in *Frasier*,
for example, seems to spend his time almost entirely at levels 1
or 2. This is a major element of his personality – a combination
of laziness and irresponsibility means he is never much
concerned about anything at all. Being laid-back to the point of
being horizontal could even be seen as his defining characteristic. Certainly virtually all the humour surrounding him arises
directly from this. At the other extreme, we have Basil Fawlty
of *Fawlty Towers*, in a permanent state of high tension. Clearly
this man has other obvious characteristics – he is a snob
(though not as much as his wife), authoritarian, tactless and so
on – but it is his continual tension which, above all, defines
him. Everything else happens within the context of the awful
tension that he carries with him, a tension so strong that it
seems to imply a massive frustration about everything he has
done with his life. Here, too, the humour arises directly out of
the tension level, in this case both the attempts to control the
pent-up tension and also its inevitable release. When in one
episode he takes to whipping his car with a tree branch, while
yelling at it as though it were a child who had dreadfully mis-
behaved, we laugh because behind the absurdity there is a

psychological truth, a terrible tension and frustration in the man which have to find some sort of outlet.

So it can be useful when making notes for a character to ask about a general level of tension. The examples I have given above are extreme, but you may decide that a particular character is, for example, generally calm (though not as near comatose as Simon). Or the character may be volatile (like Mel Gibson's Riggs in *Lethal Weapon*, particularly in the first of the series of films). Tension – and how it is handled, and where it has come from – can be a very useful starting point for the creator of character.

Use of language

This is a huge subject, and I really have to recommend to the reader my previous book *Writing Dialogue for Scripts*. How a character uses language is, of course, a major key to the character's personality. Language is not only a means of communicating but also a way of thinking, and at the same time it betrays (to varying degrees) class, age, race and geographical position, as well as attitude and status within any given conversation.

Briefly, then, in making notes about a character's use of language you might like to categorise very roughly in two parts:
1) Background: class/ gender/ age/ race/ geography
2) Style

Background

We have already dealt with background in a general way above, so at this point the creator of character need only make a note of any particular background element that is disproportionately apparent in the character's language. For example, some young people talk in language that is perfectly comprehensible to the rest of humanity, but others use language which underlines the fact that this is a young person speaking. Sometimes this is just the natural result of being part of a subculture, while in other characters this 'youth-speak' seems to be positively employed to exclude those who are not part of that group. If your character might speak like this, make a note of it. Similarly class may or may not have a particularly strong effect upon language, as may race or region of origin. Make a note of the exceptional.

Your earlier notes, then, will in general be sufficient guide to the effects of background upon the character's use of language; here you need only note the exceptional. The effects of class, say, on use of language are fairly obvious. The real danger is not of ignoring the effects but rather of over-emphasising them, having all upper-class characters talk like twittish friends of Bertie Wooster and all southern English working-class characters talking like extras from *Oliver!* As ever, subtlety and writing against type are invariably more effective than stereotyping.

When it comes to gender, however, the effects upon use of language of being male or female are not quite as obvious. Researchers have, in fact, found significant differences between the two: women tend to use language more supportively and less competitively than men, tend to make fewer attempts to dominate conversation and to make less frequent contradictory (as opposed to supportive) interruptions. Again, you do not need to note this against every female character, but it is useful to bear it in mind, and to note if there is a particular character – male or female – who demonstrates these tendencies to an exceptional degree.

Style of speech

Style of speech is a very personal matter. It is not merely a question of our background being reflected in our language, since if it were only that then all of us from the same background would talk in the same way, and very obviously we don't. How each of us talks is individualised in all sorts of ways, and these can be present in the speech of the characters we create. Briefly, here are a few of the options:

Coherence/incoherence
Is this character at home with the language? Under normal circumstances, is he or she coherent, comfortable with words and enjoying their use, or not?

Let us compare the following two speeches from Harold Pinter's play *The Birthday Party*. First, here is Goldberg, telling his companion McCann how to relax.

> GOLDBERG (*sitting at the table, right*). The secret is breathing. Take my tip. It's a well-known fact. Breathe in, breathe out, take a chance, let yourself go, what can you lose? Look at me. When I was an apprentice yet, McCann, every second Friday of the month my Uncle Barney used to take me to the seaside, regular as clockwork. Brighton, Canvey Island, Rottingdean – Uncle Barney wasn't particular. After lunch on Shabbuss we'd go and sit in a couple of deck chairs – you know, the ones with canopies – we'd have a little paddle, we'd watch the tide coming in, going out, the sun coming down – golden days, believe me, McCann. (*Reminiscent.*) Uncle Barney. Of course, he was an impeccable dresser. One of the old school. He had a house just outside Basingstoke at the time. Respected by the whole community. Culture? Don't talk to me about culture. He was an all-round man, what do you mean? He was a cosmopolitan.

In the following Act we have this from Stanley:

> STANLEY You know what? To look at me, I bet you wouldn't think I'd led such a quiet life. The lines on my face, eh? It's the drink. Been drinking a bit down here. But what I mean is... you know how it is... away from your own... all wrong of course... I'll be all right when I get back... but what I mean is, the way some people look at me you'd think I was a different person. I suppose I have changed, but I'm still the same man that I always was. I mean, you wouldn't think, to look at me, really... I mean, not really, that I was the sort of bloke to – to cause any trouble, would you? (*McCANN looks at him.*) Do you know what I mean?

Goldberg's speech is that of a man comfortable with words; he uses their power. The first few lines, for example, are made up of short, pithy, sentences, each a statement of incontrovertible fact. He does not hedge his statements with qualifications, the ifs and buts of uncertainty (or of intellectual rigour): he makes bold assertions. And then he relaxes, chatting away with confidence about his past. His sentences are not always grammatically precise, but then most people speak ungrammatically much of the time, and his meanings are never in doubt. Then towards the end of the speech there are some rhetorical questions about how cultured his uncle was, questions with more than a hint of aggression, as though attacking McCann for something which (at least as far as we know) McCann has not actually said. Goldberg is a man who likes to be in charge, and here he is using language to put McCann on the back foot – even though McCann is his own accomplice.

Stanley's speech reflects a very different character. Here, too, there are a number of rhetorical questions, but without any of the aggression, without any of the certainty behind them. And many of the sentences here are not merely ungrammatical; rather, they are on the point of disintegration. Phrases – and, we suspect, thoughts themselves – go unfinished. Forthright declaration is replaced with repetitive searching for truths that can be held onto. In fact, Stanley appears to be confused even about what he means to say, as he begins by stating that, judging from his appearance, one would probably think he had *not* led a quiet life, and ends by stating that, judging from his appearance, one *would* think he had led a quiet life, and had not caused any trouble. He seems not to realise the contradiction and, partly as a result of the hesitant and repetitive manner of speech, we may well not realise the contradiction either. But then what we take from this speech is not the meaning, in the simple sense, but rather the fact that it is very important for this character to believe (or at least attempt to believe) that he has a clear, unchanging entity at his own core. The hesitancy, repetitions and confusions are not coincidental; they in fact underline the uncertainty at the core of this character, an uncertainty which he is desperately trying to deny.

Here we have, then, not merely two speeches but two different styles of speech reflecting two very different characters. It could be argued, of course, that taking two speeches out of context is inevitably unrepresentative, as any particular speech always happens at a particular *moment*, in particular circumstances, and the character may speak in very different ways in other circumstances, at other moments. There is, of course, a great deal of truth in this – the same individual will certainly speak in very different styles when addressing the family at Granny's birthday get-together as opposed to when out in the pub with mates, and we shouldn't try to make our created characters speak in the same way all the time. Nevertheless, it is still the case that certain characters will *in general* speak in ways that are distinct from the ways in which other characters speak.

I have argued elsewhere* that dialogue in any given script exists within the particular *world* of that script, and that dialogue is not merely a matter of being true-to-life but also works (or fails to work) within the conventions that are established *within that particular script*. There is not space here to develop this theme, but we can certainly see that Goldberg and Stanley inhabit the same world. While the language of each indicates certain characteristics of each, at the same time the two speeches have much in common. In the most general terms, there is in each of them an element of the unexplained, the uncomprehended, and both inhabit a world of aggression and fear. At a more mundane level, neither speech gives much hint of the speakers having had a great deal of education, and the vocabulary of each is fairly limited, though a couple of words – 'impeccable' and 'cosmopolitan' – imply a little more breadth on the part of Goldberg. Even here, though, there is something slightly awkward, slightly inappropriate, in the use of the word 'cosmopolitan'. Goldberg likes to use such words, but they are used with a lack of precision – he is a man who thinks he knows more than he does. And while the incoherence of Stanley is obvious, Goldberg's speech, too, betrays a mind that does not move in clear lines, either in terms of meaning or emotion. He moves from relaxation technique, to memories of holidaying, to the culture of his uncle. Each of these topics does have a connection with the previous one, but the mind is in fact

*Rib Davis, *Writing Dialogue for Scripts*, A & C Black, 1998

meandering, moving with no clear purpose from one topic to the next. The speech is held together by Goldberg's strength of belief in his own opinions rather than by any logical argument.

Levels of coherence and incoherence, then, can be fruitful areas to explore when creating a character.

Colour

By 'colour', I here mean language that is coloured by the word or phrase that is not straightforward and literal, speech that uses simile, metaphor and other devices of verbal dexterity to make it more vivid. Some people delight in the use of colourful language, while others positively avoid it. In creating a character, you should ask yourself where on this spectrum this individual is placed. In the two extracts above, for example, there is very little use of colour. Goldberg does speak of his holidays coming round 'regular as clockwork' and refers to 'golden days' but neither phrase rises above the commonplace or cliché. In fact the use of cliché as colour can be used to imply a certain pretentiousness in a character, as here. Stanley's speech, on the other hand, may be entirely devoid of colour but it is also devoid of any hint of pomposity.

To take one of thousands of examples of colour in Shakespeare, in *Romeo and Juliet* Tybalt fairly innocently remarks that Mercutio 'consort'st' with Romeo, meaning he is often to be found with him, but Mercutio insists on finding the other meaning of the word, thus giving himself an excellent opportunity to take offence:

> MERCUTIO Consort? What, dost thou make us minstrels? And thou make minstrels of us, look to hear nothing but discords. Here's my fiddlestick; here's that shall make you dance. Zounds! consort!

Mercutio displays both his aggression and sharpness of mind not merely through his actions but through his dextrous use of language, moving from one to another meaning of 'consort', through to minstrels, thence to discord – both musical and physical – and finally on to his 'fiddlestick', which is, of course, his sword. This is not simple, direct use of language, but language which through its wilful manipulation of an image is not only a demonstration Mercutio's character but *is* his character.

For a very different use of colouring in Shakespeare, let us turn to Cordelia in *King Lear*. Her speech is direct and, in contrast to her sisters, devoid of artificial colour, though it is not grey, being coloured with restraint – 'I cannot heave/My heart into my mouth'. This is a character who is above all honest, and colour in language can imply a clouding of the truth, a fuzziness round the edges. There is no fuzziness in her reply when she is asked what she can say to demonstrate her love of her father: 'Nothing.' And a little later she explains herself:

> CORDELIA   I yet beseech your majesty,
> If for I want that glib and oily art
> To speak and purpose not – since what I well intend,
> I'll do't before I speak – that you make known
> It is no vicious blot, murder, or foulness,
> No unchaste action or dishonoured step,
> That hath deprived me of your grace and favour,
> But even for want of that for which I am richer,
> A still soliciting eye and such a tongue
> That I am glad I have not – though not to have it
> Hath lost me in your liking.

Here Cordelia (and possibly Shakespeare too) makes plain a belief that cleverness with words – 'that glib and oily art' – can be seen as the antithesis of honesty. Certainly when we create a character who flourishes words around, the audience may well be suspicious of such an individual, and the audience may be right. When we create a character capable of spinning and colouring the world, we should be aware of the impression that may be given.

The verbal tic
The verbal tic may be anything from the repeated 'You see' or 'like' to ending every statement with, 'Know what I mean?' Usually the tic has not been consciously learned, but occasionally something like a verbal tic has been consciously acquired. There is a delicious example in *Her Big Chance*, one of Alan

Bennett's television series *Talking Heads*. Lesley, a less than successful actress, recalls an interview for a part:

> He said, 'Forgive this crazy time.' I said, 'I'm sorry, Simon?'
> He said, 'Like 9.30 in the morning.' I said, 'Simon. The day
> begins when the day begins. You're the director.' He said,
> 'Yes, well. Can you tell me what you've done?'
> I said, 'Where you may have seen me, Simon, is in *Tess*.
> Roman Polanski. I played Chloë.' 'I don't remember her,'
> he said. 'Is she in the book?' I said, 'Book? This is *Tess*,
> Simon. Roman Polanski. Chloë was the one on the back
> of the farm cart wearing a shawl. The shawl was original
> nineteenth-century embroidery. All hand done. Do you
> know Roman, Simon?' He said, 'No, not personally, no.'
> I said, 'Physically he's quite small but we had a very good
> working relationship. Very open.' He said that was good
> because Travis in the film was very open. I said, 'Travis?
> That's an interesting name, Simon.' He said, 'Yes. She's an
> interesting character, she spends most of the film on the
> deck of a yacht.' I said, 'Yacht? That's interesting, Simon.
> My brother-in-law has a small power boat berthed at
> Ipswich.' He said, 'Well! Snap!' I said, 'Yes, small world!'

We will return to this extract later, but for now we should just note that within these few lines Lesley uses the director's name, Simon, seven times. She learned to use it this frequently on the advice of a handbook. A warning to all of us. She also repeats the word 'interesting'. Both these verbal tics are manifestations of her wanting to appear closer to – and more in empathy with – people than she really is, whether this Simon or Roman Polanski. The tics, then, are not arbitrary: they arise out of other elements of her character. Lesley, a less than celebrated actress, is continually trying to persuade both herself (seemingly with some success) and others (with less success, though she clearly does not realise it) that she is of some standing. The verbal tics are consonant with her attempting to find connections where there are none, as between a woman on a yacht, in a film, and her brother-in-law having a small power boat at Ipswich.

Really repetitive verbal tics in scripts are generally reserved for minor characters, as continually hearing the phrase can just become plain annoying. However, pet phrases repeated only a few times by major characters can be very telling. In the film *Nadine* (writer, Robert Benton), for example, Vernon Hightowers will frequently end a conversation with, 'Trust me', though we really have little reason to do so. At the end of the film, though, Nadine takes control of affairs, and she now says 'Trust me.' Taking over this little verbal tic has a gentle symbolism.

Pastimes and passions

Humanity is hugely varied. It is both entertaining and more true to the world as we know it if some of this variation is reflected. Part of the great success enjoyed by the Coën brothers is as a result of their realisation of this. So, does the character you are creating have a real passion for something – rock-climbing, collecting beetles, cultivating roses? On the most mundane level, a character having a passion for something will often provide interesting or unusual settings for scenes, but more importantly the passion itself tends to reveal other aspects of a personality: what does rock-climbing say about someone, as opposed to collecting beetles?

Many elements of our lives – and thus of the lives of fictional characters, too – seem almost pre-destined, resulting from the time, place and position we are born into. But our pastimes and passions are, at least to some extent, a matter of choice. There are limits on the choices, of course – the refuse collector will simply not be able to afford to take up show-jumping, for example – but, nevertheless, the choices that characters make in how they pass their free time say a great deal about them. And remember, having a passion for something may or may not be directly connected to expertise: it is perfectly possible to have a passion for, say, playing the oboe, without ever being good at it.

So, what does the character really love doing? What is it that they most look forward to? What turns them on? It might be playing the drums, twice-weekly clubbing, going to football matches or collecting model trains. Naturally, there will be some characters who appear to have no particular passions at all; they go to work, come home and watch television, and occasionally go down the pub. These characters are fine – there are many such people – but a script inhabited solely by such individuals will have to compensate strongly in other ways if it is to hold the attention of the audience.

It should be pointed out that here, under 'passions and pastimes' I am not including relationships. Some characters certainly appear to live for other people – it is frequently said of some parents that they live for their children – and as a result these characters spend much of their free time servicing others. This is extremely important for such characters, but should not stop us from asking what else either does excite them, or used to. A person who is always at the service of another is very often suppressing his or her own needs, his or her own passions. Working out what these might be (or might have been) can offer new opportunities in characterisation, particularly if the character then breaks away from the role of server.

Delusions

Many and varied are the ways of making a script dull. One of the most effective is to have everything be exactly what it seems to be. In this type of script the characters say what they mean; they are understood by the other characters, too, to be saying what they mean; the audience, in turn, understands that the characters say what they mean and are understood by the other characters to be meaning what they are saying. Everything is absolutely clear. The audience is given no work to do and might as well go and have a snooze (in fact may very well do so). Of much greater interest is dialogue – and action, for that matter – which demands that the audience do some of the work. In dialogue and action of this type, there are always unspoken aims lurking beneath what is said or done, only partly recognised emotions slightly blistering the smooth surface of relationships, unacknowledged goals quietly shaping words and deeds. And the audience has to work out what's going on. Of course, if the audience is seriously overloaded with the work of making sense of the production then that, too, might lead to turning off and having the snooze, but making the audience do a certain amount of work is absolutely necessary, because it is involving. This is a major ingredient in making the audience active, keeping the audience as *part* of the production. The gap between, on the one hand, what a character says and does and, on the other hand, what we as audience are actually coming to believe about that character, is the gap that we delight in filling. It is that gap that we are filling when we are working out what people are really up to – and why – in a thriller, and it is that gap, too, that is often a vital part of making comedy work – filling the gap can often make us laugh.

In terms of characterisation, one of the major gaps which can be exploited is that between what a character believes about him- or herself and what we believe about that character. Here we are not talking about lies or any outright deceit, but rather about self-delusion. We have already noted this in terms of class, but it can be much broader than this. If we refer again to the extract from *Her Big Chance* on page 48, we find that much of the humour – and pathos – arises out of Lesley's deluding herself. She is surprised that the director appears to be confused, and reminds him that *Tess* is a film by Roman Polanski, but it is left to us, the audience, to fill in the gap, knowing – as she doesn't – that *Tess* was based on a Hardy novel. She has had a walk-on part in the film, but believes herself to have had a 'working relationship' with Polanski; we fill the gap, realising that there was no relationship at all. And Lesley clearly believes that she is impressing the director who is auditioning her, as when she mentions the shawl of 'original nineteenth-century embroidery. All hand done.' Again, we fill in the gap, which is not just that we do not find this impressive (or even relevant) but we know that the director will not be in the least impressed either. The whole passage would have been far less successful had Bennett made the director deliver a number of put-downs to Lesley – she would then only have become pitiable, with all her vulnerability immediately exposed, and we would not have laughed; but by instead having the director (we later find out he is not even a director anyway) keep his opinions to himself, and allowing Lesley to keep her self-belief intact, Bennett keeps open the gap that allows us to be amused by her since, after all, she is not (yet) coming to any harm.

So when creating a character, one question we might like to ask ourselves is, is there any way in which the character is self-deluding? She doesn't believe she can become a top pianist – is she massively under-estimating her own ability? He thinks he is the most popular man in the neighbourhood – is it really true? A couple believe themselves to be stunningly attractive – are they deluding themselves and each other? Where can we open up the gaps?

Characters who delude themselves, who have *beliefs about themselves* which do not match up to our sense of reality, are a fairly extreme case of the creation of a gap to be filled by the audience. Much more common are the subtle nuances of word and action – ambiguities which keep the audience working to decide *why* a character has said or done this. And more often than not, we conclude that the motivations for little words and deeds are strongly connected to the motivations for big words and deeds. So we need to sort out the really big motivations, the really big *wants*.

This leads us on to central motivation, which could be dealt with here, as the final section of Part 1: Notes for Creation of a Character. After all, in talking about beliefs and delusions we have already found ourselves, inevitably, discussing motivation. But motivation is also very closely intertwined with the workings of plot. So it is at this point that we find ourselves moving almost imperceptibly across the line, no longer dealing with character primarily as the separate, individual character, but rather examining how character functions within a script.

Part 2: Character within Script

5. Character Motivation and the Plot

Summary

Before moving on to the major topic of motivation, let's review the notes we may have made so far. These can be categorised as follows:

Birth marks
    Gender
    Race
    Class
    Family background
    Name

Learning through experience
    Education
    Abilities
    Own family
    Sexuality
    Back-story

What the character is now
    Age
    Occupation
    Friends and enemies
    Appearance
    View of the world
    Beliefs
    General manner
    Sense of humour
    Tension levels

Use of language
    effect of background, and of gender
    personal style, including – coherence/ incoherence
                               colour
                               the verbal tic
Pastimes and passions
Delusions

Objectives and super-objectives

Our notes so far, then, have allowed us to create much of what our characters are, but have not focused squarely upon their most important attributes – their objectives and super-objectives. The objectives and super-objectives of your major characters should be central to the shape of your script, so let us be clear about exactly what they are. So far as drama is concerned, the terms originate from the great Russian theatre director, teacher and theoretician Konstantin Stanislavski. His main concern was with acting and directing, but his insights are very useful for writers, too. Stanislavski stated that when confronted with a script an intelligent actor '... ought to consider the purpose of his role, the major and predominant concern of each character, what it is that consumes his life and constitutes the perpetual object of his thoughts, his *idée fixe*. Having grasped the major concern, the actor must assimilate it so thoroughly that the thoughts and yearnings of his character seem to be his own and remain constantly in his mind over the course of the performance... So, one should first grasp the soul of a part and not its dress.'*

Stanislavski actually uses the term 'super-objective' to refer to the purpose of the whole play, the communication of its meaning and significance. The term – along with 'objective' – has also been applied not only to whole productions but, more commonly, to characters, and in particular main characters, roughly corresponding to the *idée fixe* referred to above. Objectives are what characters want to achieve, in the relatively short term. So what they do and say is to a large extent governed by their

*Stanislavski, *The Theatre of Nicolai Gogol*, pp 166–7, reprinted in Jean Benedetti, *Stanislavski, an Introduction*, p 10, Methuen 1982

objectives. Super-objectives, on the other hand, are the longer-term, overall objectives of the characters, their main aims, either in the whole of their life or within the confines of the events depicted within the script (though very often, if the script is to be really powerful, the super-objectives *are*, in fact, the major life objectives).

Sometimes it is very effective not to reveal the super-objective too soon. There is a memorable example of this in the film *The Matrix* (writers, the Wachowski brothers). It becomes established that the world is in fact only a virtual world, and humans are kept ignorant of the real nature of existence by Agents. These Agents are machines: their purpose is to destroy any humans who know that the world is only virtual. But then comes the moment when Agent Smith finally takes off his glasses, takes out his earpiece and tells the truth to his enemy Morfeus: this machine, Agent Smith, cannot stand being on Earth, it quite literally stinks. And his purpose is not merely to destroy those humans who know the truth – and specifically Zion, the last outpost of these humans. No, what we had thought to be the whole *raison d'être* of the Agents, turns out to be only an objective. Agent Smith reveals that he has a super-objective: to leave this stinking Earth and be free, and it is only in order to achieve this super-objective that he must achieve his objectives. Suddenly a whole new layer is revealed in this mechanical character: he had been harbouring a super-objective, and one arising out of an emotional need.

When it comes to dealing with a character's objectives within a particular scene, then these objectives would not normally figure within your character notes, but would certainly be at the forefront of the mind when writing the plot synopsis (and, of course, when writing the script itself). But the super-objectives which govern the *general* direction of a character's actions should certainly figure within the character notes.

Threaten it

In real life, though, our super-objectives are often not at all clear. I would not find it easy to state my own super-objectives. For the most part we may well feel as if we're just bumbling along quite happily without giving 'super-objectives' a second thought, or even a first thought. But they exist nevertheless. 'To be a respected member of the community' might be a super-objective, or 'To bring up a happy family'. Such super-objectives may seem so ordinary – even boring – that little of interest could arise out of them. Wrong. A play or a film is not merely a slice of life (most slices of life are fairly tasteless). What a play or a film does is to make the protagonist – and in turn the audience – experience the super-objective as it has never experienced it before. It brings it into focus. One basic way of doing this is by threatening the super-objective. So, a particular character wants above all to be seen as a respected member of the community? Threaten it. Drag up something from the dim and distant past, something disreputable, and see how far the character will go to achieve the super-objective. Or have someone make up lies about what this character has been doing, and see where this leads, see what this apparently ordinary individual is willing to do to protect a hard-earned reputation.

Super-objectives are the things we live to attain, and we may find ourselves crossing all sorts of emotional, moral and even legal thresholds to reach them. The more obstacles you as the writer put between your protagonist and the protagonist's super-objective, then the more you test the protagonist, forcing him or her to drive the story along in order to achieve the super-objective and at the same time revealing more and more of what the protagonist is made of. This character wants above all to bring up a happy family: what threatens that? It could be a malign intruder into the house, but that might only produce a straightforward, predictable conflict. What about looking more closely at how the Happy Family is to be achieved: perhaps the protagonist is determined to hold it together despite the protagonist's partner's repeated affairs. The super-objective is thus threatened, and where might that lead, in plot terms? Or what about the protagonist imposing a particular model of Happy Families, such as everyone always having to do everything together? Or alternatively giving the children complete freedom because that way lies happiness? How do the other members of the family react? Do they threaten the protagonist's super-objective (because of the way in which it is pursued)? And then we may be led to examine what is behind the character's super-objective. Is the Happy Family really there for the sake of the members of the family, or is even the protagonist made to confront the fact that this super-objective is, in fact, all about appearing to be the perfect parent and partner, for others to admire and – above all – for the protagonist to admire in the mirror? The most fruitful super-objectives, then, may not be as simple as they seem.

Being super-supered

And super-objectives can change, or at least appear to change: they can be super-supered. To take a simple example, a character's super-objective is, let's say, to get rich. Her objective (her route to the super-objective) is to get the stolen gold; but ultimately she is faced with having to either give up the gold to other criminals or be shot; she gives up the gold. Her super-super-objective turns out to be staying alive. This staying alive is, we may suppose, the super-super-objective of all of us. But, to take a contrasting example, a protagonist's super-objective may be to hold on to the family company in order to pass it on to his children, but in fighting off an attempt to take over the company he finds himself sinking further and further into the immoral methods of his rivals, ultimately leading to the disgracing of an innocent individual who has become unwittingly involved in the intrigues. On realising what he has done, the protagonist commits suicide: his over-riding objective turns out to have been living with honour.

So, in reality, there are whole hierarchies of objectives and super-objectives (and, if we want to call them that, sub-objectives), which might even seem bewildering. As a writer, though, it is nevertheless useful to reach a simple decision – for the purposes of the script – as to what is each character's super-objective. It is sometimes said that a character should only have one super-objective (or even that it is impossible for a character to have more than one super-objective). Of course, if one defines super-objective in a certain way (as the single over-arching objective of the character), then this is necessarily true. And it is certainly the case that, for clarity, many scripts work very well on the basis of the protagonist (and usually the other major characters as well) having that one, clear super-objective. My own opinion, however, is that while the concept of the single super-objective is extremely useful, we must take care not to allow it to constrain the character too much. If almost everything that a character says and does is too clearly aimed towards that super-objective, then we have only suc-ceeded in finding a new route to the creation of flat characters. Very often, in fact, the super-objective is something that is imposed on a script once it has been written, partly because that seems to help the actor, who might otherwise feel lost. As writers we must use the super-objective as a unifying force within the process of characterisation, but not at the expense of complexity.

Despite these reservations, it is also true that when a protagonist's super-objective is not sufficiently clear, or is not sufficiently central to the plot, the script can suffer.

Let us take as an example the film *Pink Cadillac* (writer, John Eskow). The protagonist (Clint Eastwood) is an ingenious if unenthusiastic hunter of people who have jumped bail. What is his super-objective? It appears to be to have a quiet life. This is threatened by a woman who he is meant to capture but with whom he becomes emotionally involved instead. This leads to his defending her in a shoot-out and then reclaiming her baby for her (it has been captured by a fanatical fascist group). But much of this is not driven by the protagonist's desire for a quiet life (if this is indeed his super-objective). He becomes moti-vated, rather, by his wish to help and defend his new-found partner, and this, in a vague way, seems to be his new super-objective. As to the fascists, the villains of the piece, well he certainly disapproves of them, but his (successful, of course) sortie against their camp is not primarily motivated out of opposition to their actions and beliefs, but rather is merely a part of the recapture of the baby. This is a pity: there is insufficient connection between what the fascists do, and the actions and motivations of the protagonist: they happen to be fascists, and he doesn't like them, but that is really incidental. In short, there is a somewhat messy vagueness about his motivation and how it relates to the other elements of the piece. The film is pleasant and diverting, but lacks the power that it might have had, had the protagonist's super-objective been clearer.

This is not to say that a super-objective may not change (though the purists in this area might argue precisely that – that it does not change). If we take, for example, the character of Mr Allnut (played by Humphrey Bogart) in *The African Queen* (writers, James Agee and John Huston) we are again presented with a protagonist whose super-objective appears to be to lead a quiet life, even if that does entail trading up and down a river in a war-torn part of Africa. The threat, as in *Pink Cadillac*, comes once more from a woman (Rose, Katherine Hepburn) with whom he begins by having a business relationship which then leads on to an emotional attachment, against his better judgement. This time the change of super-objective is much clearer, and indeed the change itself is a major element of what the film is about, whereas in *Pink Cadillac* it goes almost unremarked. He becomes as determined as she to avenge the death of her brother and to do all he can for the war effort, so his confrontation with the enemy is not incidental but is a statement of his new super-objective.

So your protagonist's super-objective can certainly change. Indeed, many scripts are about a voyage of self-discovery (more of which later), through which the protagonist finds out their true super-objective. But for the script to function as well as possible that change should be a clear one, and should also be central to the new direction of the plot.

The great fear

There is another way of looking at central motivation: this is to start not from the super-objective but from the great fear. What is it that your character fears most? It could be that he or she has some secret buried in the past, a secret that could destroy them. Or, more subtly, it may be a fear of some characteristic of theirs. Perhaps, like the aggressive neighbour in *American Beauty* (writer, Alan Ball) it is a fear of his own sexual preference; it is this fear that drives him to such fury against his son whom he (mistakenly) believes to be homosexual, and it is the unintentional exposing of his own sexuality which leads to the climax of the film. Or, as in *Othello*, the fear might be that, despite all his great achievements, the protagonist is not certain of his own attractiveness to a beautiful woman, because, in part at least, he is black and she is white; his great fear is of being cuckolded. To identify a character's greatest fear is the flip-side of identifying a character's super-objective (in fact avoiding the realisation of a greatest fear can be interpreted *as* a super-objective); either of them can be the driving force behind a character's actions, and in turn the driving force behind a script, for they are both about what the character most wants.

What you want, what you really really want

In his remarkable book *Games for Actors and Non-Actors*, the Brazilian director Augusto Boal makes a distinction between 'character' and 'characterisation'. Boal defines 'character' as being essentially static, but 'characterisation' as dynamic: 'character' is basically a description of what a person is like, including their background, etc., but 'characterisation' is much more than this, because it includes the essential ingredient of *will* – what the character *wants*, and wants are what carry the action forward, making things happen. (Here he is developing Stanislavski's belief that character is not a state, but active.) Boal goes on to say that it is not enough simply to want in the abstract: for our purposes a want has to be very specific. It has to be to marry this particular person in these particular circumstances, to avenge the death of this particular person in this particular place, to make it to the top of this particular company at this particular time. It is the *wants* of a character that bring an otherwise static individual to life; it is the *wants* that produce action.

The counter-will

Boal recognises, though, that *wants* are not simple, and this leads him on to discuss the importance of what he calls the 'counter-will':

No emotion is pure or constant in quantity or quality. What we observe in reality is quite the reverse: we want and we don't want, we love and we don't love, we have and we don't have courage. For the actor to truly live on stage, he must find the counter-will to each of his wills. In certain cases the counter-will is obvious – Hamlet wants only one thing, to avenge his father; but on the other hand he doesn't want to kill his uncle. He wants to be and not to be. Will and counter-will are concrete and obvious to the spectator. The same phenomenon applies with Brutus, who wants to kill Julius Caesar, but struggles inwardly with his counter-will, his love for Julius Caesar. Macbeth wants to be king, but he hesitates to assassinate his guest.

... Let me stress again: if an actor is to play the role of Romeo, he must love Juliet, sure, but he must also look for his counter-will. Juliet, however beautiful she may be, however adorable and amorous, is none the less a minx at times, an irritating and stubborn little girl. Juliet must have similar reservations about Romeo. And because they also have counter-wills, their wills must be even stronger, and love must explode with even more violence in these two human beings made of flesh and bone, of wills and counter-wills.*

Boal is mainly directing these comments to actors, who must always find the counter-will in the character they are playing, but the observations are just as apt for the writer. If the writer fails to imply a counter-will, then the resulting character will be two-dimensional, flat. There must always be an element of conflict *within* the character, quite apart from the conflicts between characters. (Naturally, though one may disagree with Boal about the precise nature of the counter-will in both Romeo and Juliet, these two characters actually seem quite blindly focused upon the positive qualities of each other. While it may be useful for actors to try to envisage counter-wills in terms of their direct feelings towards each other – as opposed to the

*Augusto Boal, *Games for Actors and Non-Actors*, translated by Adrian Jackson, Routledge 1992, p. 55

internal conflicts arising out of their strong family loyalties – there seems to be little or no evidence for this in the actual script. Of course, such counter-wills may have existed in Shakespeare's character notes for the roles – we will never know.)

Sometimes this internal conflict is very obvious – as in *Hamlet*, as Boal points out – but at other times much less so, but any character who feels no reservations whatever about his or her central wants is ultimately a less interesting character, a less rounded character, even a less credible character, and a character with whom we as audience are less likely fully to engage.

Of course, this all has to be explored by the actor, but if the material to start with has no depth, no counter-will, then the actor has a decidedly uphill struggle. How often have we come out of a theatre or cinema commenting that so-and-so did not really act very well, only to realise later that the fault lay in the flatness of the script – there was simply not enough for the actor to explore. And how often have we credited an actor with a fine performance, when just as much credit was in fact owed to the writer for the creation of a truly complex character, contradictions and all.

The complex character

Some years ago I wrote a BBC radio play entitled *Can't Complain*. The initial idea for the play came from a chance meeting I had with a woman who would not stop talking. It was virtually impossible to know what was truth and what was fantasy in what she said, but she was an immediately memorable character.

> DOLLY You know, I was going to buy a round of drinks like, got me money with me, all ready to buy a round of drinks. For Billy and that. Nice lad he is. You do these amateur dramatics do you? Good they are. Meet people. Got to, haven't you? But it's a nice place, Felsham, I'm not saying that. But you got to, haven't you, otherwise, you know, you might as well snuff it and no-one'd know the difference. But I'm all right, you know, got lovely kids,

five lovely kids. After my first husband – first one that is – after he'd moved on like, I got married to this builder. Not really married, you know, one of these registration offices. Anyway, I had five of his. Could have been more only a wall fell on him. All but done him in. Big strong fella he was, but it almost done him in. Should have done. But I had five of his. Can't complain, can you? Eldest, she married this Italian. (*proud of the word:*) Restauranteur he is. Got a line of 'em. Only they like it when I go down, you know, give 'em a bit of good English cooking, bacon and egg and that. They like that, don't eat nothing decent, so when I go down there they're saying, 'Mum, give us some of your cooking.' So I do. Well you've got to, haven't you. Go down there all the time, I do. Always a welcome. Can't complain. Five I had, only then a wall fell on him. Bit of a cabbage he is now. Smiles a bit, dribbles a bit, that's about it. Big strong man he was.

I was pleased with the creation of this character. If she seemed somewhat extreme I didn't mind at all, as I knew that the woman I had met was just like this, never listening, hopping from one vaguely related topic to another, apparently unclear even in her own mind about what was true, what was embellishment and what was pure make-believe. She was also quite funny – or, rather, was the source of some humour (though I was aware that the humour must not be cruel, as could easily have been the case) – and a character bringing humour is always a plus. So, for me, the character worked. She became the protagonist of a play in which all sorts of people tried to help her, or at least dealt with her, but she was only forced into some sort of compromise with reality when she met another person as irrational and unpredictable as herself. The play was duly broadcast, but I began to be increasingly aware of its weaknesses, chief amongst which was the character-isation of the central character, Dolly. Here was a character so vivid, so unusual, that it had never occurred to me that any-thing more was needed. But, in fact, she was two-dimensional. Not only did she provide no surprises after her initial appearance, but there were no real indications of any other elements of her character that were not immediately implied by that opening speech, quoted above. There was no complexity. And, because there was little that she was really aiming for – her super-objective was not at all clear – the play had a static quality. Despite my attempts to build a plot round this character, the script never really took off, as it was never really going anywhere. I had been dazzled by a character (actually, by a real person) and thought that that was enough. It wasn't, and isn't.

By way of contrast, let us reflect upon the character of Little Billy (Gene Hackman) in the film *Unforgiven* (writer, David Webb Peoples). Here is a man of savage brutality, a cold and ruthless villain willing to maim or kill anyone in his way. His super-objective is clear: to control his community. And yet this same man is devoted to the completion of a house he is building. This is where his thought goes, where his love goes. And he can be quite lyrical about it. In addition, it is as though building this house should somehow entitle him to respectability, as if it somehow wipes away his other actions. Indeed, when he finally meets his end he manages to say – apparently more in surprise than anything else – that he was building a house. It is as if this ought to mean that he can't possibly deserve to die, or at least not yet. In wanting to complete his home, he is wanting to be able to sit on the veranda, in his old age, and watch the sun set over the stunning landscape. He says as much, revealing that he has a vision of the future which many of us can identify with, and at the same time showing that he can appreciate beauty. His might be a clichéd dream, but it is such a powerful one that it almost seems to justify his existence. It is as though in some strange way he were building the house on behalf of all of us, and so it is that he feels such astonished injustice when his work is interrupted by death. He is not even very good at building – his house keeps falling apart – so, despite ourselves, we find ourselves in a strange way warming to the humanity of this individual. Of this killer. It is this element of Little Billy's character that turns him into a three-dimensional creation, when otherwise he could so easily have been a mere cardboard villain. We may even be left thinking, 'If only...' – if only he had taken a different turn somewhere a long long way back, he might even have been a good man. There are still traces of the good man visible. They fascinate, they intrigue. But a flat character would have left not even the faintest 'If only...', for a flat character feels as if he or she could never have been anything else; there are no hints of the might-have-been, there is nothing to imply that this individual could ever have been different or could even have been seen differently.

In calling for complexity, then, while recognising the central importance of the super-objective I am also calling for the contradictions, the counter-will, and perhaps the unexpected, that make us fully human beings, and show that each of us just might have been something else.

Character and plot: an organic process

In making our notes up to this point, we have for much of the time been dealing with the creation of character as though that process were virtually divorced from a particular script, or even from a particular script idea. For the most part, we have been assuming a process which starts from the creation of character and then moves on to the creation of a script. This is, of course, very far from how successful scripts (and thus successful characters) usually come into being. Often, in fact, they come into being in something closer to the opposite order, starting from a story or plot, with this then leading on to the fleshing out of the characterisation. The very best working practice, however, is the hardest to reflect in the structure of a book like this, for it is organic, with both plot and character developing together. Perhaps the starting point is a story idea, and it immediately becomes clear that for the story to work it will have to have a particular sort of character at its centre; then as that character is developed, an element of it suggests a new direction for the plot. And so on. And this is just at the planning stage. When it comes actually to writing the script, once again this is not just the script equivalent of painting by numbers. As you write, the characters seem to take on lives of their own, and although you have at least rough plans (and possibly quite precise plans) for what they are to say and do and when they are to say and do them, the characters don't always obey. And nor should they. At the moment of writing the scene you are breathing life into the characters, into their conflicts, their feelings, their desires, and if that really is life that you are breathing into them then at times – like any living creature – they will surprise you. And, at that moment of writing, you must allow it to happen. You mustn't tie the characters down completely or they will resent it, and refuse to really live for you at all – they will just stand around pretending to be alive, and everyone will see the pretence. So at least for now, you must listen to them, watch them, and go where they take you. After all, when you have finished typing for the day you can always go back and say, 'No, no, no, you're not going there! What a ridiculous idea!' and re-work the whole sequence more in line with what you had in mind in the first place. On the other hand, you may decide that this new, uncharted (and unplotted) territory into which your characters have led you is actually quite fascinating, revealing new complexities in relation- ships (really living characters do tend to have complex relation- ships) and new possibilities for character development, and it might be worth your while adjusting the plot to accommodate this. As the God of your script, ultimately you are in command, but it's only fair to let your characters have a bit of free will as well. It's all part of the organic – not mechanical – process.

So if that organic process is how your finished script (and thus, of course, your complete characters) might eventually come into being, then a character's objectives and super-object- ives cannot be considered simply as a matter of characterisa- tion, somehow as though it were separate from the plot. *The central character's objectives and super-objective should be the driving force behind the plot.* Plot is not just a matter of one thing happening after another; plot is about how one event is inextricably tied up with another event, and the ties that bind these events are, above all, the motivations of the characters concerned. So when we sit down and plan the super-objective of a central character, what we are really planning is the motor for the plot. Or, if we start at the other end, when we map out a plot, that has huge implications for the super-objectives of the central characters.

On the other hand, you may not be interested in creating a plot. You may be happy with a fairly aimless story, where the

characters are jiggling puppets to which things continually happen for no particular reason, and where the ending could occur
just as appropriately at one point as at another, since the piece
is not bound together by the motivations and goals (fulfilled or
otherwise) of the characters, so there is always room for
another onslaught of events. In such a script, the characters are
kept fully occupied in *reacting* to an endless string of occurrences, since nothing springs from their own needs. The plot –
such as it is – is divorced from the characters, so could take
place pretty much as easily with one set of characters as with
another. The plot, here, is what happens and the characters
simply people the plot. You may be happy with this – actually
a story rather than a plot – but finding a producer who is
equally easy to please might prove more difficult.

Plot-driven, character-driven

These terms, 'plot-driven' and 'character-driven' are often used,
particularly in the context of film. Their meanings are fairly
obvious: a plot-driven script is one in which *events* are primary,
and it is to a considerable extent the job of the characters to
react to the events. The plot may be very complicated, with
continual knock-on effects of one event upon another, and even
all sorts of intrigues, but while these intrigues may be at least
to some extent arising out of the wants of the characters, the
impression is nevertheless given that the characters are there
essentially to serve the plot. Character-driven scripts, on the
other hand, are those in which the exploration of character is
central, with the plot arising out of this.

That, then, is the distinction between the two categories;
very often, though, where the script is of any real quality, the
distinction is not a real one. A film like *No Way Out* (writer,
Robert Garland), for example, may seem to be plot-driven.
Appalling things happen to the protagonist (played by Kevin
Costner): the woman with whom he is having a secret affair is
killed; he only finds this out when he is handed a photograph
of her and is put in charge of an investigation to find her killer;
evidence is found which is bound to implicate him eventually
in her death, so he has to deflect attention from this; his boss

(in charge at the Pentagon, no less) has also had an affair with the same woman and our protagonist knows that the boss probably killed her, but he is duty bound to protect his boss as well; he is forced to protect the dead woman's friend, who is almost killed by men employed by the villain... and so on. Certainly the protagonist has to react to all of these events (and many more), but there are two major redeeming features which render the term 'plot-driven' inadequate for this film. Firstly, these events are not a matter of simple misfortune: they are not Acts of God, but arise directly out of the objectives and super-objectives of the other major characters, particularly the villain, who is also a subordinate of the protagonist's boss but who, we later learn, also has an extreme devotion to him arising out of a closet gay passion for him. Secondly, the protagonist himself has a major hand in shaping events: while he has a great deal to react to, he also makes things happen of his own accord. He takes the initiative to protect his dead lover's friend, for example, and also takes the initiative to confide his great secret to his closest friend (although that leads to the friend's death). More importantly, the task he is given – carrying out the investigation – arises out of the character he has created for himself (we find out at the last that he is in fact a Soviet agent): brave, honest, trustworthy, highly intelligent and totally dependable. And his very involvement with the dead woman in the first place turns out almost certainly to have been not accident but the result of her also being the mistress of his boss. This is very clever plotting, mechanically speaking, but it is more than that: it is a plot that arises out of the super-objectives of the characters even before we realise it. The writer manages to convince us of the protagonist's motivations even though they turn out to have been in fact subsidiary to his super-objective of not being discovered as a Soviet agent. And at the same time he is taken on an emotional journey (more of which in the following chapter): we are always concerned about him as a person, not merely as a pawn in a plot. At the end, we find out his real motivation for involvement with the woman, but still there has been no mistaking his very real feelings for her. On his dis-covering that she has been murdered we witness him being physically sick – an act witnessed by no other character and therefore not for their benefit. His emotional involvement is absolutely genuine, and it is this which leads him at the finish to question who he really wants to be – whether he is able to continue as a Soviet spy, or even as a Soviet citizen. Characterisation has at least in part acted as the motor for the plot, and the plot in turn has driven the protagonist on an emotional journey. In writing of quality, then, 'plot-driven' and 'character-driven' are not so easily to be distinguished: character forces new turns into the plot, and plot reveals new layers and new directions for character.

A character in three acts

Having emphasised that the distinctions are often not real ones, however, it is also the case that in extreme cases a script may be justly categorised as plot-driven, and in such cases the outcome is unlikely to be entirely satisfying. And in other instances the drive of the piece seems to change halfway. A criticism that has been levelled against the excellent film *Billy Elliot* (writer, Lee Hall) is that it changes drive in the middle, the first part being essentially character-driven (the plot arising out of young Billy's super-objective to be a ballet dancer) and the second part being essentially plot-driven (the characterisation failing to move on, leaving the plot to do the work). This type of divide is, in fact, quite common, as the first part of a script is naturally more likely to contain exposition, a setting-out of character from which the plot can arise, while the second part usually feels the right place to develop the action arising out of that exposition. There is then very often a third, much shorter part, which is some sort of resolution of the conflicts which have been explored in the earlier sections. This is the classic three-act structure familiar to playwrights and screen-writers: set-up, development and resolution (which seems to be common to other art forms as well: in music, it roughly corresponds to the sonata form structure of exposition, development, recapitulation). A thousand different ways have been found for a script to present this form and to play with it, with action teasers coming at the start and codas at the end, with flash-backs to reposition parts of the exposition into the develop-

ment and double endings to throw the last part of the development into the resolution, but in all its guises the three-act form
remains the most popular structure. One of the problems it
poses in terms of characterisation, however, is that it can lead
the writer to explore character in the first act, successfully implying the central motivations that lead to the action, but can
then lead the writer to overlook further significant exploration
and development of character in the second act, while, instead,
developing only the plot. Then there will often be some 'learning'
in the brief final act, the resolution. But that is not enough:
characters' objectives and the conflicts between them should
continue to be the driving force behind the development of the
plot *through the second act*. Plot should not be allowed to take
over entirely.

Back-story

As we mentioned in an earlier chapter, back-story is the set of
important events that have happened before the 'now' of the
action. It is important to come back to it once again here, as it
can play a major role in the revealing of character, in a way
that has a particular effect upon plot.

What we consider 'back-story' and what we consider merely
'story', or 'plot', depends on where we decide to place the 'now'
of the action. It also depends on the weight and import of the
back-story. In *Citizen Kane*, for example, is the whole of the
action showing Kane's life back-story? Of course not: it is, after
all, the bulk of the film. It is the plot, seen from a perspective
after the protagonist's death. And yet that perspective is vital,
that perspective that struggles to find out who J. F. Kane really
was. The attempt to discover the truth, after his death, is also
the plot, and in fact it is the relationship between these two –
the 'real' life of Kane and what is later discovered about him –
that produces the tension holding the film together, and keeping
us in it. 'Back-story' is usually used to *explain* actions that take
place in the 'present'. This applies in *Citizen Kane* as well, but
also in reverse: the action of the present is an attempt to explain
what might otherwise be considered back-story. It is only the
two together that reveal the character of the protagonist.

But in most plays or films it is much clearer when an element is 'back-story'. This is the simple result of the placing of a 'beginning' before which everything else is 'back'. Thinking in characterisation terms, how should the writer decide upon where to place the beginning? A story is a series of events. Why not simply start when the events start? The problem is, one event is always the result of another (and this includes, of course, the start of the protagonist's life: we might want to know where and when the character was conceived; and then we might want to know why, and so on); we could keep going back for ever. Usually, the choice is made to start from a point (or close to a point) where the central conflict arises. We might then, later, go back to find out more about the background of the characters. Back-story is usually not so much a laying-out of events that happened in the past – though it often is that as well – as *a laying-out of how character traits were acquired*.

Let us take as an example Jack Rosenthal's famous television play *Spend, Spend, Spend*, the construction of which produces a very large amount of what we might (just – there is almost too much of it for the term to be appropriate) call back-story. It starts with the protagonist, Vivian, and her husband Keith being presented in public with a huge cheque; they have won the pools. We move from here back to Vivian's childhood. She is a tough young girl because she has to be, living in poverty, stealing bits of coal to sell so that her bullying father can go out and spend the money on drink, as well as looking after her four brothers and sisters. And she learns that she can't always afford to be loyal to her long-suffering mother. From here we move back to the present, with Vivian and Keith in the luxurious hotel bedroom, already surrounding themselves with expensive purchases. The contrast between back-story and present makes each much more vivid.

We move to back-story again, with Vivian in poor clothes, clearly uncomfortable with herself and her inability to attract boys. This goes some way to explaining the fury we have just seen her vent on her husband, in the hotel room, at his having looked at the legs of the high-kicking girls kicking right in front of him at the presentation. Still in the back-story, we see that in her desperation Vivian has stolen a manicure set from her grandmother. She is pitifully anxious to look good. We see her braving her father's blows to wear a short skirt and lipstick. She dreams of Mr Right. And when her father lights a fire in the grate, thus (unknown to him) burning to a cinder the precious manicure set, which must have cost all of a few pence in Woolworth's, Vivian tells us that that box was the most beautiful thing she had ever seen. And, she says, it still is. Here, with this direct connection being made between the then and now, we have the best use of back-story. It is not there merely to fill us in on a bit of personal history. Rather, the back-story always throws light on the character *now*, and the character experiencing the events of now. Here is Vivian, with her fortune, looking back on that cheap manicure box, and we can see that, in one sense at least, money isn't going to mean a great deal to her.

Back to the present, and Vivian and Keith trying to cope with intruding reporters and neighbours. They are at Vivian's parents' house, and the moment Vivian has been waiting for arrives. They tell her mother that they will be giving her five hundred pounds, but then when her father virtually asks what he will be receiving, Vivian and Keith delight in telling him: nothing. And we already know why. If Vivian seems at this moment a cruel and heartless character, we understand why, through the back-story. Vivian's father proceeds to smash the place up.

After another section of the present, dealing with begging letters, we have more back-story, Vivian in bed with a man. We learn that she enjoys physical contact with this man, Matthew, becomes pregnant and soon marries him. But almost immediately she realises that she doesn't love or even like him. She is unhappy, frustrated, resentful. One night she sets fire to the sofa. What sort of a person does that, we might ask ourselves. A person with a father like hers. And at this point it is the 'present' that is informing the character we are seeing in the back-story. The best example of this particular type of violence from her father is what we have just seen in the 'present' – his smashing up his own house out of fury and frustration. But clearly he has always been like this, and Vivian has always been learning.

Vivian complains to us that Matthew didn't even stop her burning the sofa. And he didn't complain when she told him that she kissed other men. He was just happy if she was happy and, she tells us, that selflessness is obviously no way to go about making a real marriage. Again, previous back-story has shown us the model she inherited. And when we see her yelling at her child, we know where that came from, too.

Back to the present. Vivian (her hair now green) is adoring her new Chevrolet, despite the fact that she can't drive. And she visits the factory where she had been working, as they still owe her a week's wages. She is indulging herself, and even rubbing it in to those around her, but, since we know her background and suffering, we allow ourselves to maintain our sympathy. We hear the neighbours' criticisms (Vivian and Keith now have a new house), we see that the car is never washed but just sits there, and see that Keith is only interested in going drinking. We might have an attitude towards these characters similar to that of the neighbours, except that the back-story has prepared us to feel pity rather than contempt. Characterisation is not merely something the writer concocts about a character in the head; rather, it is what the writer *makes the audience feel* about the character. Characterisation is not merely the attitudes produced in the character but also the attitude produced *in the audience*.

More back-story. With Vivian's marriage coming apart, she starts to see Keith. Her eyes lighting up at the prospect contrasts with the character of now: now, her eyes only light up at *things*.

Back in the present, the newspapers are finding as much muck as possible to print about the couple, and piles of begging letters have turned to piles of threatening letters. The following back-story presents her lying to Matthew about a rendezvous with Keith. This is interesting: the effect of the back-story here is actually to *diminish* audience sympathy with Vivian. Perhaps the newspapers (in the present) have a point. The back-story is filling in the unpleasant side of her character. And yet somehow we still know enough of the reasons for her desperate need for some sort of happiness – she's never had any in her youth. We still allow ourselves to retain warmth towards her.

In the present: such are the threats that Vivian now wears (ridiculous) disguises. She is sinking into illness, and depression. She and Keith have become totally isolated. Even the Doctor fails to help her. This scene is juxtaposed with one of passion from her early days with Keith, a scene which becomes horribly comic when his grandmother arrives and searches the house for him. The scene then takes another turn, as Vivian vents her frustration: the grandmother had ruined something genuinely beautiful, one of the few such moments in her life. Again, we learn more from this about the character in the present, and her pain at having nothing really beautiful now.

Back-story: Vivian and Keith go on holiday, and while in Tangier she gives chocolate to the children who are – as she observes – in greater poverty than she has experienced. Here the back-story allows us to appreciate that, despite her not replying to the begging letters in the present, she is not mean, nor uncaring. Probably she simply didn't believe them.

In the present, in her fury at the prying neighbours, Vivian throws a brick through one of their windows. We already know where that character trait was learned. They move to a different area. Similarly when, later, Keith hits her but it doesn't occur to her to leave him, we know where she first took in that pattern – both from her father's hitting her mother and hitting her. Vivian said she somehow loved her father even then. So now she continues to love her husband.

The back-story finally catches up with the point just before that where the play began. With four children now, Vivian is in real poverty, experiencing hunger, eating whatever scraps she can, indulging in shop pilfering to eke out an existence. And her mother refuses to continue helping out looking after the children. Vivian and Keith splash out their last tiny remaining money on beer.

Keith sits downs with his pools coupon to hear the football results. We are expecting this to lead to sudden, wild celebration. Instead it leads to sudden death. We cut straight to Keith's corpse in the car that he has crashed yet again. The shocking incongruity between what we expect and what we get, between this piece of back-story and this piece of present, makes a statement in itself: hearing those pools results leads straight to his death. And there is Vivian, miserably looking at his body. She has swapped one misery for another. Only then do we cut back to Keith hearing more of the pools results, and the pathos is almost unbearable. The back-story informs the present: these are two characters who have never had much control over their lives, and when they receive an amount of money that ought to represent freedom, in fact they find themselves with even less control: they can never escape their upbringings.

The final intercutting sequence between past and present alternates between Keith's growing tension, disbelief and jubilation at having forecast draw after draw, with Vivian's driving the Chevrolet, frantic, alone, grief-stricken. And then she is bankrupt, working as a stripper singing *Hey Big Spender!* Taking us through Vivian's further marriages – to number 5 – and disasters (all gleefully reported in the press) the remainder of the script is all in the present. The ending, though, pulls back-story and present together, and is worth quoting at length. She goes back to the street she lived in when she was first married to Keith, and gently cries. Across this, we hear her voice (from a present more recent than the 'present' of the play):

VIVIAN [*voice over*] I looked. And I remembered everything. I thought if Motherwell had got another goal and Stockport not drawn with Oldham... we'd still be there. Happen we'd have had the front room furnished by now. With its nice glass doors. To let the sunshine in.

They always say never look back. But sometimes it's the only way to *see* yourself. And it's then I understand why everything went wrong: because there was no *other* way it *could*'ve gone.

Maybe it's all my own fault. People like me aren't much good. You know, a bit sick. But there's *others* as bad. Happen a bit of it's *their* fault. Bank managers and news-papermen. The only difference is – *they* make a living out of it...

Money's a mystery to people like me – and Keith. The more you bugger up your life, the more they like it. [*Pause*] Did you say you like a good laugh? Here's a good'un for you... when we won the pools, we put a cross on the coupon for No Publicity.

I had some bad times in that street. *Bloody* bad. So bad I wanted to die. [*A beat*] They were the best times I ever had.

6. The Emotional Journey

Your central character – or characters – should travel an emotional journey. *So should you, the writer.*

It has often been said that writers need to love their characters. That is because it is true. It is said with almost as much frequency that there should be a bit of the writer in every character. That, too, is true. But what does it really mean? What it means is that, as you write the character, as you write the script, everything that that character says and does – and what every other character says and does, too! – must be mentally said and done, too, at the moment when those words (of action or dialogue) go on to the page. However well planned in advance a character may be, that character has to be *lived by you* as you write the part, as you write every part. Whether hero, villain, whatever, and whether the action at that moment is morally good, bad or indifferent, it must be lived by you – through you – at the moment that the action hits the page. You must feel what the character is feeling, and allow yourself intuitively to enter into the motivation (however appalling) and feelings of the character at that moment. This is what should be meant by loving the character. We have to love the character in the sense that we have to love ourselves. It is sometimes said that if we knew enough about anyone we would forgive them for what they do; we have to forgive the character, and more – we have to be *on the side of* that character, seeing things utterly from his or her point of view. Obviously you can't *be* that character, but what is demanded is more than mere empathy, more than mere understanding, and certainly more than planning.

While I am writing, members of my family often mock me. There I am, tapping away at the computer, and yet quite unconsciously I am mouthing words, stopping to make gestures, grinning to myself, making threatening faces or even laughing. I am experiencing what the characters experience. It looks a bit daft, I am told. But I believe that if you don't completely enter into each character, if you only try to empathise *from the outside* then the characterisation will never really work. It will never really take off.

I should emphasise that this applies to *every* character. It is not enough to enter into the life of only your protagonist, or even your other prominent characters. You must live the experiences of all the individuals who feature in your script. This has to be done at the actual moment of writing, but then, when you finish a scene, it is sometimes useful to read it again *focusing particularly on just one character's lines and actions*. Of course, when doing this it would not be sensible to cut out everything else that others say and do, as many of the lines and actions of any one character are totally bound up with the lines and actions of others, but just focusing upon one character can help us to be sure that there really is a convincing *through-line* for that character, that that character is not *only* responding to others but also has a genuine independent existence through the scene.

Emotional identification

It is only if you, the writer, have complete identification with your characters, that then the audience will identify with them, too.

Much is often spoken about certain characters in plays and films being 'easy to identify with'. This is usually put down to these characters living in circumstances which many so-called ordinary people recognise, and having problems that many of the public also have to deal with. A play about the bullying of a child, say: many of us as either parents or children have had experience of dealing with this. Or a film about a man or woman's guilt at betraying a partner, and yet not being able to stop themselves: many of us have been there, too. But there is a basic misconception here. In order for the audience to identify with a character, it is not in fact necessary to place that character in a specific situation that is instantly recognisable by the audience. What is important is to place the character in an *emotional situation* that is instantly recognisable by the audience. If we place Tom Hanks on a desert island (*Cast Away*) and see how he gets on, we are not inviting the audience to compare that with their own most recent desert island abandonment, or even with their last holiday in the Caribbean. The protagonist here is being put in an *emotional* situation, and this is much more important than the physical one (although, of course, in this case it arises out of it). So he is having to deal with isolation: many of us have experienced that. He is having to evaluate his life – the choices he has made, his achievements and failures – just as many of us have felt the need to do at times of crisis. He is facing the imminent possibility of death, again as many of us do. And he is having to see what resources he has within himself – emotional resources, above all – to cope with his circumstances. The situation may be an extreme one, but the *emotional* reality is what counts, and it is that which we can identify with. If it were only a matter of our identifying with his attempts to make fire (our memories of camping expeditions, being a Scout or Guide) then the identification would be pretty thin. Of course, the fact that a strong emotional reality has been established does not in itself guarantee that this will be a good script – we may have various opinions on *Cast Away*, for example – but it is certainly a good start.

Conflict and development

One of the most useful pieces of advice I ever received was to think of good drama as 'the development of character through conflict.' I have always held on to this. The protagonist – and where possible other major characters as well – must develop through the script, and the means of that development taking place is conflict.

But why should your characters (or at least your protagonist) develop? Why should we not be content with characters who are fixed as what they are, and merely collide and bounce off each other? Well, sometimes that is enough; it depends on the genre. In a James Bond film, for example, we do not expect genuine character development. There is a certain amount of *character exploration*, certainly, but if there were to be much real change in the characters – and the serious audience consideration that this would call for – we might feel rather uncomfortable. We hadn't come here for this, after all. We had come here to hear 007 say 'shaken but not stirred', we had come to see if there would be a bike chase over a glacier or through a desert, we had come to see The Beautiful Girl (or, now, The Feisty, Independent, Beautiful Girl), and we had come to see lots of clever gadgets and big explosions. We had not come here to see character development. Fair enough. Most of us can enjoy James Bond films, and many other films like them. (There are also television series in similar style, but far fewer stage or radio plays). The fact remains that in anything remotely more demanding (and this includes many comedies, of course), character development – a character changing, or showing the potential for change – remains a vital element in scripts.

But why? The first answer, I think, is that it gives us all hope. Let's take the film *Pretty Woman* (writer, J. F. Lawton) as an example. There is the prostitute, plying her trade on Hollywood Boulevard: she has nothing; there is the business tycoon, clinching multi-million dollar deals: he has everything. But she does not have nothing: she has an intuitive grasp of right and wrong, and asks questions. And he does not have everything: a workaholic with another failed relationship behind him, he gains little satisfaction from his achievements. Both characters begin to change. She gains in confidence; he learns to take time away from work and enjoy simple pleasures. She begins to see what she could become, and turns down his offer of being his kept woman – an offer she would have jumped at even a week earlier; he changes his whole way of operating, deciding to contribute something to the economy and society at large: he is now going to be building great big ships, rather than just stripping assets. Finally, she has altered so much that she decides to be a prostitute no longer. And at the very end of this fairy tale, when he comes and saves her, she tells him that she will be saving him right back.

Now what does this all represent? How does this (hugely successful) film work? Simply: the destitute prostitute, the unhappy millionaire, they can both be changed. And we all fall somewhere in that spectrum between these two extreme characters, so we are all catered for. We can all be changed. We can all find happiness.

And it is not only that the circumstances can change (as they certainly do for the prostitute); the more important alteration is in the minds of the characters, as they discover their potential. This is what we all want to do. We all want to change, none of us is totally happy with who we are, with the lives we are living. Furthermore, the agent of change (through conflict, but we will come on to that) is each other: they are altered and saved *through a personal relationship*, and isn't this, too, what we all want? Plays and films show us that all these things are possible, but most important of these is the possibility of change itself.

Scripts like *Groundhog Day* (writers, Danny Rubin and Harold Ramis) and *Sommersby* (writers Nicholas Meyer and Sarah Kernochan, a remake of the French film *Le Retour de Martin Guerre*) go one further: these present us with the possibility of change through, in effect, taking on a different life. In *Groundhog Day* the grumpy, cynical protagonist develops through having to live the same day over and over again. He wants to win the heart of his colleague but his own insincerity and unpleasantness get in his way. Through the constant repetition of the same day, with his learning each time what his mistakes lead to, he gradually develops. His conflicts are resolved; he makes the right choices; he gets the Girl. We can all live in hope. In *Sommersby*, on the other hand, the protagonist simply takes over the life of another. This is a man who wants to reform, but normally would never get the chance. Here is the chance: despite the secret sins of his past, he now is given the opportunity to develop. It ends in tears, naturally, but it is a very moving script: we would all like to be given a second chance, wouldn't we? The chance to start again, to make the choices and develop as we should have done.

Of course, characters do not always accept change. At the start of Ibsen's *A Doll's House* Nora is the sweet accommodating wife, happy to devote herself to husband and children in return for a variety of pet names and a little status.

> HELMER (*from his room*) Is that my little skylark twittering out there?
> NORA (*opening some of the parcels*) It is!
> HELMER Is that my squirrel rustling?

NORA Yes!

HELMER When did my squirrel come home?

NORA Just now. (*Pops the bag of macaroons in her pocket and wipes her mouth.*) Come out here, Torvald, and see what I've bought.

HELMER You mustn't disturb me!

Short pause; then he opens the door and looks in, his pen in his hand.

HELMER Bought, did you say? All that? Has my little squanderbird been overspending again?

By the end of the play there has been a huge change: she has rejected all her former values and is striking out on her own. (And this is what was so shocking to Victorian audiences – the idea of a woman actually making choices that would allow her to change!)

NORA (*undisturbed*) I mean, then I passed from Papa's hands into yours. You arranged everything the way you wanted it, so that I simply took over your taste in everything – or pretended I did – I don't really know – I think it was a little of both – first one and then the other. Now I look back on it, it's as if I've been living here like a pauper, from hand to mouth. I performed tricks for you, and you gave me food and drink. But that was how you wanted it. You and Papa have done me a great wrong. It's your fault that I have done nothing with my life.

HELMER Nora, how can you be so unreasonable and so ungrateful? Haven't you been happy here?

NORA No, never. I used to think I was. But I haven't ever been happy.

HELMER Not – not happy?

NORA No. I've just had fun. You've always been very kind to me. But our home has never been anything but a playroom. I've been your doll-wife, just as I used to be Papa's doll-child. And the children have been my dolls. I used to think it was fun when you came in and played with me, just as they think it's fun when I go and play games with them. That's all our marriage has been, Torvald.

Not only has Nora changed radically, then, but she even *understands* the nature of the change, its causes and, it emerges a little later, its possible consequences. It is this knowledge of the nature of her personal emotional journey, and its implications for the whole of society, that is so threatening, to Torvald Helmer and many others then and since. Torvald calls on her to honour her sacred duty as a wife and a mother, to be guided by the teaching of the Church, to follow some sort of morality, and finally he declares, of course, that she must be ill, out of her mind. But Nora is not out her mind, and realises that the two of them cannot possibly stay together now:

> NORA You and I would have to change so much that – oh, Torvald, I don't believe in miracles any longer.

That is a testament to how far she has travelled. But her husband, Torvald Helmer, who is also given the opportunity to change, steadfastly refuses to do so. He cannot understand what has been happening to Nora, let alone accept that he might need to change himself. And we know that he won't change – through the whole play he has not given the slightest hint that he could – but still he is given the opportunity and we wish he would take it. That option is important, for it is not only what our characters *do* that matters, but also what they *could do*. We may not like Torvald very much (though at the time the play was written there must have been many in the audience who would have held nothing against him at all) but we can still put ourselves in his position, and can still live out his choice. Giving our characters the *opportunity* to change is almost as important as having them actually change.

Conflict and choice

But why conflict? Why may character not develop through other means? The answer lies in the link between conflict and choice. Our lives develop through our making choices: we choose this path and not that. The choices we are faced with are always to some extent in conflict with each other: we cannot at any one time be both a highly paid executive and a worthy social worker; we cannot marry both this man and that man; we cannot be both thief and honest person. (Though actually there are a number of memorable films and plays which explore the idea that indeed one might somehow be able to lead just such double lives. But these scripts don't ignore or avoid the matter of choice, they merely look at it from another standpoint.) We all have to make choices between conflicting demands, or conflicting possibilities. Sometimes, of course, the choices we make – should I eat the jam or the honey? – are of no importance, but the choices we give to our characters in drama should be of real significance: at best, they should have the potential to change the characters' lives. And not only do we force the characters to make those choices, but we put the audience in the position of making the choices as well. When watching a play or a film we are continually wanting to tell the characters what to do – indeed, it is not unknown for the audience to offer advice out loud! (In children's theatre the audience, having fewer inhibitions than adults, need very little encouragement to shout out both warnings and advice.) And this making choices on behalf of characters is very involving, pulling the audience closer and closer into the action, which is precisely what needs to happen if a script is to be successful.

If you are in any doubt as to the drawing power of choices, just watch Caryl Churchill's double play *Blue Heart,* and in particular the first half of it, called *Heart's Desire.* This consists of one little scene being run over and over again, but on each occasion it is different. Sometimes the change is totally unexpected, the result of events over which none of the characters appear to have had any control, but many of the other deviating versions arise out of one or more of the characters having made a different choice at some point, or a number of different choices, resulting in utterly disparate conclusions. In the very first version, one of the speeches is about the various directions that evolution might have taken, so that now instead of seeing ducks and water rats and moles we might see some creature combining characteristics of each of them. This, we come to realise, is a metaphor for the play – we are seeing how things might have been, and then how they might have been again. We are never told which of the scenes is the 'real' one – they all are as real or as unreal as each other (though some of the funniest or most bizarre – including gunmen bursting in and killing them all, or a horde of small children rushing in, running round the room and then out again – are quite hard to make sense of; if these things are to happen, then all sorts of other circumstances must have been different). The whole play explores our fascination with the might-have-been, the ways in which – with just a different choice having been made here, or there – our lives could so easily have been altered beyond recognition.

As remarked earlier, there are both internal and external conflicts. The external conflicts are usually against other individuals (or sometimes groups of individuals, though making the conflict *personal rather than theoretical* is usually a good idea). They are not necessarily physical conflicts, of course, but are usually conflicts over some form of power, ultimately controlling the destiny of the protagonist. There may also be conflicts with creatures – rogue whales and sharks come to mind – or, more commonly, against forces of nature, as in, for example, *The Perfect Storm* or *Twister*. But in every case, whether the conflict is against another individual or, say, the freezing Andes (as in the film *Alive*) *the script will succeed only to the extent that the external conflict is internalised.* If *The Perfect Storm* (writer, William B. Wittliff), for example, is something less than the perfect film, it may be because the convincing conflict really is only against the waves: there is not enough going on *inside* the protagonist. Where there is little or no internal conflict, all the audience can do is take sides. Sometimes taking sides is quite difficult, or quite fun (a few of us may have been rooting for the Sheriff of Nottingham rather than Robin Hood in *Robin Hood, Prince of Thieves*) but usually it is not a hard choice: we side with the good guys; and in *The Perfect Storm* there are not many of us who are going to side with waves the size of an office block. So while in a film like this there is conflict, there is little opportunity for the audience to get involved in making choices, so interest in the protagonist – and even in the whole piece – is severely diminished.

This is not to say that a script may not both call upon the audience to take sides and offer internal conflicts – most of the best films do just that – but it is always the latter that are crucial to character development.

There may well be other cultures in which conflict is not seen as the driving force behind drama – or indeed behind many of the workings of society itself. In the West, though, perhaps it is as a result of our predominantly Judaeo-Christian heritage that we tend to see our existence in terms of opposing forces, particularly Good and Evil, and these opposites produce *action*. In music we have discords and clashes of keys which are called upon to be resolved and even in visual art a canvas is not seen as static – certain lines, colours and shapes *draw* our eyes from one point to another. In drama, similarly, there is action and conflict and we want resolution, but once that resolution is achieved then that is the end, we can go to bed now. That is what we usually mean when we say that a play or a film sags in the middle: there has been a temporary apparent resolution. The writer may know that new conflicts are brewing, but the audience doesn't, and as the characters seem to be sorted out the audience feel they can go to bed. So, in plot terms, there must always be an element of conflict, and if one conflict appears to have been resolved then another area of conflict must still be active. In character terms, this means that ideally there should always be an area of *internal* conflict, calling on us to make choices on behalf of characters.

Choices lead to learning

We learn more about characters through their *actions* than from anything else, and their actions result from the choices they make. These in turn arise out of conflicts. A character may appear to be kind and good, until faced with a decision which then shows him or her to be selfish or even completely lacking in scruples. Some choices show humanity in a very harsh light: many films set in Nazi Germany, in particular, reveal how much can be learned about characters when they are faced with choices involving the lives and deaths of others.

In general, the choices – and conflicts – which confront our central character should be of increasing severity as the script moves on, revealing more and more of the character.

Let us take Shakespeare's *Coriolanus* as an example. The conflicts faced by the protagonist are at first merely physical ones – he has battles to win, and he does so tremendously impressively. Neither he nor we are aware of any internal conflict here, and even though we meet the enemy we feel no particular empathy for him, so we simply take sides, and as we are seeing the drama from Coriolanus' point of view, it is his side that we take. From early on, however, both his enormous pride and his contempt for the common people are entirely apparent. Here we might find ourselves siding with the people, although Shakespeare does his best to present them as a fickle rabble. Then, when Coriolanus is called upon to display his wounds and call upon the common people for support, as was traditional for one destined to become Consul, he chooses not to:

> Better it is to die, better to starve,
> Than crave the hire which first we do deserve.
> Why in this wolvish toge should I stand here,
> To beg of Hob and Dick, that does appear
> Their needless vouches?

The choices he makes arise directly out of his character (and we are given ample evidence of the forming of his character through meeting his imperious and blood-lusting mother, Volumnia). We may well feel split – even more split in our feeling than he is: given how the common people are presented, we can understand his despising them but, on the other hand, why should they all be battle heroes? Would we be? And shouldn't the people be entitled to be addressed with respect? So the conflict pulls us in, inviting us to make choices on behalf of Coriolanus.

When he has made his attitude perfectly plain, the people turn against him and refuse to name him Consul, leading to fury on both sides. His mother then presses him to swallow his pride and speak with humility to the crowds. With Rome now in turmoil the stakes have been raised, the conflict is greater and the choice more important. Coriolanus chooses to be meek and mild with the commoners as his mother requests, but when it comes to the deed he cannot carry it out – he can neither control his anger nor rein in his arrogance, and for attacking the common people he is banished.

The next choice facing Coriolanus is of even greater magnitude: whether or not to join forces with his erstwhile foe, Aufidius, General of the Volscians, against Rome. He decides to do so, and in making this decision reveals his own priorities: ultimately his loyalty is shown not to have been to his own land after all, but rather only to a part of it, the Senate – or perhaps, we think, his only real loyalty is to himself.

The final and most momentous choice with which he is faced comes at the gates of Rome itself, when his wife and young child and then his mother come to call on him not to attack the city. It is his mother, still, who finally has an effect upon him, having kneeled down to him. Coriolanus must choose, between the entreaties of his family, and the expectations of his new allies (coupled with his desire to seek revenge on those who banished him). Coriolanus chooses not to attack the city, instead pressing for peace between Rome and the Volscians, although knowing that this may well be fatal to himself. All that he has done in his life, it now becomes clear, has been to attempt to please his mother, his mother who since his childhood had delighted in his brutality, and later had taken pleasure in hearing whenever he had been wounded, and it is to his mother that, ultimately, he feels allegiance. The great, the proud, the arrogant Coriolanus, most terrifying warrior of his day, is finally found to be a creature of his mother. And it is indeed this final choice of allegiance that leads to his death.

Choices defining identity

In *Coriolanus*, then, each conflict and each choice is of greater magnitude than the last; there is a continual 'upping of the ante', leading to the final, identity-defining climax. This last phrase, 'identity-defining', is important, for in many of the finest scripts this is what the protagonist discovers – their true identity. Towards the end of Arthur Miller's play *The Crucible*, Proctor is faced with the terrible choice of either signing to false involvement in witchcraft or facing death. He sums up his own awful dilemma with the heartfelt cry, 'God in Heaven, what is John Proctor, what is John Proctor?' His choice will define who he is. Or we might turn to Sam Shepard's play *True West*: the conflict between the brothers Lee and Austin becomes a struggle over identity, with Austin choosing to tighten the cord round Lee's neck rather than have his identity stolen from him by his brother. Or there is Frank McGuinness' play *The Factory Girls*, where again a conflict – about whether or not to continue a factory sit-in – becomes a matter of who these women actually want to *be*. Or we may turn again to *The African Queen*, with Mr Allnut desperately holding on to his identity as the lone and somewhat reprobate bachelor; he defends his habits as being only natural, famously prompting Rose to remark that 'Nature, Mr Allnut, is what we are put in this world to rise above.' His decisions, to allow himself to become romantically involved with Rose and to join her in risking all to sink the German ship, involve giving up this identity and agreeing to take on another very different one. Finally, to take an even lighter example, in the film *As Good As It Gets* (writers, Mark Andrus and James L. Brooks) the insufferably bad-tempered protagonist (Jack Nicholson) is presented with a series of choices which ultimately lead to his becoming, at least to some extent, a different person. He decides that he is capable of change, and is willing to try to carry through that change. His choices are absolutely about his identity.

Choices lead to actions

As writers, we allow the audience to learn about our characters from what they say about each other and from what they say about themselves, but most of all we learn from the choices they make, and this is because these choices lead to action. The audience learns about them from what they *do*. To go back to Stanislavski and Boal, characterisation is not something passive, but active. People *do* things, and for scripts the old saying holds true: actions speak louder than words. So when, in that organic process described earlier, plot and characterisation are taking shape, we must make sure that we plan enough for our character to do for the audience to find out what this person is really made of.

Your strongest, most arresting character should be the protagonist. In terms of character interest, it is important that your protagonist is not upstaged – or at least not in terms of the complete script. This means, above all, that this is the character with the strongest actions, and these actions must be *personally* important. It is not enough that someone does something that will help thousands of others; it must also be of *personal* importance to this particular character. So when, in *A Few Good Men* (writer, Aaron Sorkin) the whole dreadful system of 'code red' within the military is challenged and – at least in this instance – defeated, Daniel Kaffee (Tom Cruise) is not merely achieving something of importance for others – it is also of huge importance to himself. Not only has he come off best against the arrogant Colonel Nathan Jessep (Jack Nicholson), a formidable opponent, but – much more important in terms of characterisation and actually making the script work – it is a victory against his old self, the self we see at the start of the film, always willing to come to an out-of-court settlement, always content to take an easy route out. In fact, it is made clear that even by insisting on accusing Jessep at all, he is risking a court martial himself. Kaffee is clever with words, certainly, but it is for his actions that he is remembered.

Similarly, when in *Erin Brokovich* (writer, Susannah Grant) the protagonist (Julia Roberts) takes on a massive business conglomerate and eventually wins, this is an action of major importance not only for those on whose behalf she is fighting but also *for herself*. A single mother close to the bottom of the social scale, from the start she has a battle on her hands firstly to survive and secondly to be taken seriously, even before she becomes involved in this case. Winning does not only mean gaining something for the families of those that suffered at the hands of the polluters, but also represents success in completely recreating her own image; she gains respect. And all of this is done in extremely difficult circumstances, both domestically and professionally. The stakes are high for her personally, as well as for the cause for which she is fighting. Again, it is what she *does* that defines her character.

We should not over-simplify. The character of Erin Brokovich is not summed up simply in the statement that this is a woman who took on the polluters and won. There are a thousand other components of her character. We can easily discern her class, her probable education and other elements of her background; choices, remember, include making decisions about such matters as clothes, make-up, music and decor. And through other choices – and her actions based on those choices – we also see that she is intelligent, sympathetic, persistent, brave and willing to use her sexuality in a vital cause. It is through making a succession of such choices, and acting upon them, that characters are carried on their emotional journeys.

A journey of discovery

The emotional journey of your protagonist is very often, then, a journey of discovery, through which he or she discovers what they can become. There is a major element of change, certainly, but the change is usually from occupying one part of the potential personality to occupying another. If the change is too abrupt or too extreme, or there is absolutely no preparation for it, then we do not find it credible. We need to be able to say to ourselves, 'Yes, I can see how this character could have been like this before, in different circumstances; the conflicts and choices have simply allowed the character to discover this potential in him- or herself.' Tragedies are often the outcome of a character not being able to change enough, not being able to discover a person inside themselves who is able to cope with the events that have arisen.

In order to emphasise the length of the emotional journey it is important to position your protagonist some way away from where you want him or her to be at the start. Hence the frequency of the reluctance of the protagonist to get involved at all. Very often the central character has to be lured out of a peaceful existence to take part in the action. By the end, then, this underlines how far the character has come. In *Unforgiven*, for example, Clint Eastwood plays a man who has turned his back on a life of violence; the brutality in much of the rest of the film is thrown into even starker relief by this, and his emotional journey is even greater. Or there are the numerous gangster films that begin with the safe-blower or other vital gang member being tempted out of retirement by just one last job. Or there are the romances that start from the protagonist being a confirmed bachelor. In all these very different genres the principle here is the same: position your protagonist at the start a good distance from where he or she is going to finish up at the end.

The extraordinary play *Mud* by Maria Irene Fornes affords a good example of an emotional journey. First, we need a brief synopsis. The journey is that of Mae, a strong young woman eking out a living at the very bottom of society. She looks after Lloyd, a lazy, illiterate and sick young man whom her father (now dead) had brought into the house. Mae and Lloyd are like brother and sister, although in the past they have slept together. Despite his sickness of the liver, Lloyd refuses at first to see a doctor, and then won't take his medicine. It is not clear whether this is entirely out of fear; it may be that he wants to stay in a state that will demand the continued attentions of Mae. Mae makes a living from ironing but she is getting herself educated; she wants to better herself. Henry, a much older man, comes to live with them as Mae's partner, prompting a bitter rivalry between him and Lloyd. Henry thinks he knows much more than he does, but he is sufficiently fluent with words to impress Mae. Lloyd steals some money from Henry. Then, following an accident, Henry is paralysed; he, too, has to be looked after by Mae, and even to some extent by Lloyd, who hugely resents it. Henry now steals some money from Mae (Lloyd had never returned the money he stole from Henry). Mae finally decides that she must leave, and tells them that she is going to. Lloyd shoots her rather than let her go.

This bald summary does not come close to doing justice to a remarkable play, full of subtlety and tension, but it does serve to underline that it is the journey itself (in this case, as in *A Doll's House*, towards emancipation) that is important, rather than whether the destination is reached. If drama is generally all about conflict and choices, *Mud* is about lack of choice. Mae didn't choose the dreadful circumstances into which she was born and didn't choose to have Lloyd live with her. She felt obliged to look after him. She did choose to have Henry live with her, but really she was fooled by him, and then felt obliged to look after him, too. After his accident the unpleasantness of Henry becomes apparent, but still Mae feels she has no choice but to nurse him. It is only after he steals from her that she finally makes the choice to leave them both, to let them both survive as they may; she has a life to live. It is a play about not having choices. She is not allowed this most momentous of choices, and dies in the attempt to make some headway in her life. She has had an emotional journey, from acceptance of her lot to realising that she is having her 'blood sucked', and that she can and must do something about it. Her life is cut short, but the emotional journey is nevertheless complete.

The journey that is most effective in terms of drama is not one that follows a straight line. The plot, of course, may or may not also follow a straight line (probably not) but this should not be confused with the *emotional journey*. The plot may have all sorts of stops and starts, and these are likely to be reflected in the emotional journey, but they are not the same thing. The twists and turns in the emotional journey are mostly about *doubts* – doubts about whether the changes that are happening are right – about whether the *choices* that are being made are right. They are doubts about who the character wants to become. Often, a fairly bad guy becomes a fairly good guy, but with plenty of reservations along the way. And these are important. If the journey is too direct (the journey, that is – not whether or not the destination will be reached), if there is never any question about where it is headed, then our interest, as audience, may weaken.

7. The Emotional Journey, Case Study: When Harry Met Sally

Let us take an extended look at the film *When Harry Met Sally* as an example, examining particularly the *direction* in which the characters appear to be moving as the film progresses. Of course we have to bear in mind that this is a certain specific type of script: it is a romantic comedy and it is a film. In other genres emotional journeys might be depicted rather differently, but at the same time many of the points made here are generally applicable.

The film starts with the song 'It had to be you' and a couple of old people being interviewed about when they had first met. The old man says that at the moment when he first set eyes on his wife-to-be he turned to a friend and declared that this was the woman he was going to marry, and he did so. And here they are, many decades later, still married. This opening sets up the whole film, introducing the main characters (Harry and Sally, of course) but at a decidedly oblique angle. The song certainly supports what the old man has said, but then as soon as we meet Harry and Sally it is clear that these individuals are completely incompatible, and, unlike the old couple, they show no attraction for each other, either. So how does this fit with the song and the interview? It is as if we are being told, 'It's all right, everything will work out.' The 'It had to be you' has become 'We're going to find out that it had to be you *despite everything*!' So the emotional journeys of the two protagonists are set up, but with great subtlety.

Harry is kissing his then girlfriend, Amanda, when Sally drives up (she is giving him a lift to New York) and continues to kiss her and swap declarations of love. A song is now telling us 'Our love is here to stay.' But somehow we know, since these love declarations come at the very start, that there is an irony here; there is something not totally committed about Harry even as he is replying to Amanda – subtly, she is having to make all the running. Sally, meanwhile, puts on a false smile and hoots to show her good-natured impatience. Now, she is not impatient because she is in a hurry; rather, she is impatient with the idea of romance. She is, as she later says all women are, 'practical'. And the false smile, too, says something about her: she always tries to be pleasant, and she hides her real feelings. So, at this point, we may think the emotional journeys of these two will have very little to do with each other. Except for that opening song and that interview. And except for the title, *When Harry Met Sally*. We know from that that this film is about Harry and Sally. And we don't go to a play or watch a film in a vacuum. We have probably seen some publicity of one sort or another, so we are likely to have some sort of expectations. Part of the art of the writer is to *play with those expectations*. Meet them and don't meet them. Don't make it all too easy.

They set off on their journey to New York, Sally very sensibly proposing different ways of dividing up the driving for the eighteen hours it will take them to get there while Harry eats grapes. He doesn't just eat the grapes: he bites them straight off the bunch, then loudly spits the pips out through the open window. These characters are being set a very long way away from each other, and it will appear to get further before it gets closer.

On the way to New York Harry reveals what Sally refers to (because she has already been told about it) as Harry's 'dark side'. Harry will read the end of a book before he starts so that, should he die while reading it, at least he will already know how it finished. And he is proud to say that he thinks about death every day. Sally, on the other hand, declares herself to be a happy person. But not only are these two characters very different: they also don't get on. (After all, sometimes characters who are very different do get on: these don't.) Each tries to impose their view upon the other, in particular about the ending of the film *Casablanca*: Harry's is a romantic interpretation, Sally's a 'practical' one.

This is the point in the film when the two of them are emotionally at their most distant. Their views of life, as demonstrated by their views of that film, are poles apart, and it is hard to see either of them changing very much.

Their incompatibility is further underlined when they order food. Harry just places an order, while Sally's order is impossibly precise and finicky. Harry looks at her with incomprehension, and she just replies 'What?' At the end of the meal Sally takes out her calculator and works out precisely how much each should pay for the meal. But here for the first time we see something that is to recur: Harry appears to find her behaviour both extremely odd and attractive. But this new possible direction certainly isn't to be made definite yet – in fact it seems nothing more than a tiny aberration: Sally sees him looking at her and asks '*What*?' The two of them are not communicating clearly, and the moment passes. When, shortly afterwards, Harry 'comes on' to her (though not very forcefully) she rejects the proposition, as we would expect, and once more the two of them start disagreeing, this time Harry declaring that men and women can't be friends because sex always gets in the way. Sally, of course, takes the opposite view. The new song tells us 'Let's call the whole thing off.' They part in New York with a handshake, telling each other to have a nice life.

Let us pause to make a few observations. Firstly, these are two very strongly written characters. Sally is all controlled precision, mixed with a certain smugness (Meg Ryan sticks her nose in the air quite wonderfully); Harry is laid-back and painfully honest, even about being utterly unreliable when it comes to relationships. The writing doesn't enter the realm of caricature but both characters are extremely memorable. And to some extent we learn about them *through contrast*. Putting the two of them together (and particularly locking them together in a car from Chicago to New York) throws the characteristics of each into sharp relief. It is often the case that we only really find out about characters when we take them *out of their environment*; this allows them to make fewer assumptions than usual, to have to be more explicit. Putting Harry and Sally together is not quite like the old ploy of sticking your City gentleman in the desert and seeing how he gets on, but it does have something in common with it.

The next interview with two old people is about high school sweethearts who never forget each other, coming together decades later to become a happily married couple. Here, as in all these interviews, we are being told what might be the emotional direction of our protagonists. But it is done subtly. Harry and Sally were not high school sweethearts – far from it! – but they, too, will not forget each other. So the script is finding a way *outside of the characters themselves* of telling us what is going on inside them.

Sally now has a new boyfriend, Joe. When Harry walks past the two of them kissing in an airport, he comes back. We think it is because he has recognised Sally. It is because he recognises Joe. Given the previous interview, the script is here gently playing with our expectations. Sally seems to try to avoid being recognised. Whether Harry really doesn't recognise Sally at this point is not clear. Perhaps he doesn't, or perhaps he doesn't want to show it – better to keep a distance from this woman about whom he has ambiguous feelings.

Again there are declarations of love, but just as Harry wasn't entirely convincing in the car park with Amanda at the start, so Joe isn't convincing here in the airport. Emotionally, Sally is being taken further from Harry, but she is actually taking part in a very similar set of emotions (though on the receiving end) as Harry was at the start.

Harry finds Sally in the plane and gets the seat next to her. Harry presses to get to know her again, but Sally is very reluctant. Harry has not changed in the five years from the start. He still dreads the future. This time he tells how he never takes a girlfriend to the airport at the beginning of a relationship as, later, when things change, he won't want to take her to the airport, and, as he never wants to be asked why he doesn't take her to the airport any more, it is better not to do it in the first place. Sally, meanwhile, is ordering her food in her usual way. So they seem as far apart as ever (or perhaps further – Sally is now emotionally committed to another man), except that Harry is now *choosing* to spend time with her, as opposed to simply making the best of things, which is how his approach on the journey to New York may feel. It is only *after* Harry has made this choice to sit with her that he tells Sally (and us) that he is getting married. This is clever. We would have read the scene differently had we known this from the start. Now we find ourselves rethinking it.

There is a delicious little piece of dialogue here where Harry talks about how, after sex with a new girlfriend, men really want to get away very quickly – within thirty seconds if possible – while women want to be held all night. This, like the earlier speech about sex making male-female friendships impossible, broadens out the whole meaning of the film. The speeches express where Harry is, emotionally, but at the same time open out the whole debate about how men and women approach relationships. So while the film personalises the issues through the emotional journeys of these two individuals it also invites audience involvement and response through putting those journeys into the wider context. (In the hands of a lesser writer, it should be noted, this can be painful, 'issues' and 'meaning' being ponderously pointed out as though the audience were too stupid to see the significance of things for themselves. In *When Harry Met Sally* it is done with a wonderfully light – and, courtesy of Billy Crystal, deadpan – touch) .

Notice that the emotional journeys of the two protagonists in this film are to a large extent concerned with *each other*. This is a love story, a romantic comedy, so the writer – and the audience – is concerned with how, when and why they will ultimately get together. We have noted previously that putting obstacles in the way of objectives is the normal way of exposing character, as well as developing plot. But here the obstacles stopping these two coming together are entirely in the characters themselves, as there are no external obstacles at all (apart from the other relationships that they choose to enter into). In this piece, plot and emotional journey track each other exceptionally closely; in fact, this script is so much focused upon *character*, that the plot, such as it is, arises totally from within it.

As they leave the airport Harry, as ever, analyses to death the nature of relationships and why platonic relationships cannot work, but still wants to take Sally to dinner. Sally simply says goodbye. So the divergence is clearer than ever: he is interested (despite his intended marriage), she is not.

Another interview with an old married couple. Again this helps us to see the direction our protagonist may be headed in. The old people tell us about how they were married after a series of divorces and failed relationships. Where without the interview we might feel as if we were going nowhere, we have hope again. (The interviews also, incidentally, help us to accept the time jumps.)

It is some years later again, and over a meal Sally tells her friends that Joe and she have split up. She says she is not upset, they have been growing apart for some time. Balancing this, at a ball game Harry is telling his friend that his wife is leaving him. Unlike Sally, he is open about being upset. There is an additional little balance here, too. Sally had split up for some days before she told her friends; Harry's wife had not only known for some days that she was leaving Harry without telling him, but had actually ordered the removal men. As earlier, the two of them are going through parallel experiences, but from (at least apparently) opposite ends.

Harry and Sally bump into each other in a bookshop. (It is not a matter of chance that he is looking through a book on Personal Growth Making Life Right, while prominently displayed next to her is a book entitled Making Life Right When It Feels All Wrong; there are many ways of indicating emotional directions, and of having fun doing it). This time it is Sally's friend who helps us see a possible direction: she tells Sally that it is just like a movie where the woman says that the man is the most contemptible person she has ever met, and then they fall madly in love. This is like the writer winking to the audience: we all know what's going to happen really, it's just a matter of how.

Harry and Sally both tell each other that their relationships have fallen apart, and we then move directly to the two of them having lunch together. This is clever sleight of hand. Had we seen the invitation to the meal (and after all, it was an invitation to a meal that Sally had flatly turned down at the airport), then it would have been difficult to avoid that moment taking on a heavy significance, almost like an acceptance or rejection of entering into a relationship, but as it is this is skipped over, leaving the direction of each of them much freer, more ambiguous. For the very first time, they seem relaxed together.

Sally has not wanted to get married, but now she tells Harry that it was suddenly discovering that she did want to have children, that led to the break-up of her relationship with Joe. Sally has changed, then, but not in a way that seems likely to make a relationship with Harry any easier, as he has just emerged from a failed marriage himself. Sally, of course, says that she is convinced that ending the relationship was the right thing to have done.

The two of them walk in the park. The park: this gently shoulders a mass of symbolism. This is where people relax, where people enjoy themselves, where families go to have fun. And in the background the music is telling us the same thing. We are not given the words (and we weren't given them at the start of the film either) – that would be too crude – but it is the tune once more of 'It had to be you.' This is the start of the two of them really learning to enjoy each other's company. They chat, they joke, they laugh. Harry even manages to apologise for his behaviour of ten years previously. And Sally asks him out for dinner. This is a turning point in the relationship, in her emotional journey, so it is *emphasised by being focused around a recurring gesture*, the invitation to have dinner. Such repetitions make comparisons easier, make the shape of the developments clearer to the audience. Before, an offer had been refused; now it is accepted. There has been a change. For the first time in his life, Harry has a woman friend who he is not trying to sleep with. This is a change in him and, of course, for their relationship.

Another interview with an old couple. The old man, talking, appears not to take any notice of what his wife says, so the two of them do a lot of talking across each other. And yet despite this they are in harmony. Again, this is a pointer to the emotional direction to be taken by our protagonists.

There follows a voice-over sequence, of a telephone conversation between the two. He is clearly fairly miserable, toying with an executive toy or in his bare room, while she continues to seem self-sufficient and happy, in her office, out making precise selections from a salad bar or doing aerobics. (The moments in the office are one of the few occasions to touch on the work of either of them: we know that she is a journalist and he is a political analyst, but this script successfully ignores virtually the whole of their working existences, just as some other excellent comedies do, such as *Four Weddings and a Funeral*.) In this sequence we learn more abut their respective emotional positions from *what we see* than from *what they say*. As the voice-over continues we glimpse them out for a meal together, and his sympathy for the waiter taking her order; then she is at a mail box, checking that each letter has gone in properly before putting in the next one: Harry eventually takes the whole bunch of letters from her and stuffs them in. So not everything has changed (it would be too easy if it had): he can still be infuriated by her, even if at the same time he is becoming resigned to her ways. Through all of this voice-over telephone call, while we have been watching images of them apart and together, the two of them have separately been watching *Casablanca* on television, each in their own bed. So this sequence has so far combined voice-over with a series of images, but the conversation that had been voice-overs now become normal conversation itself, as the screen splits and we see each of them in bed, on the phone, giving their reactions to the film. This is seamless and brilliant, allowing us to see in a smooth and concentrated way exactly where they are now, emotionally.

They walk in the park again, and compare sex dreams – they are certainly becoming more intimate. But she still doesn't understand the way he looks at her. 'What?' she asks once more.

In a museum together, they are enjoying each other's company. Harry asks her to go to the movies with him. This is skilfully handled by the writer. Harry is using a silly accent, and the invitation is hidden behind it, so we are really not sure what he is feeling or meaning. Going to the movies together is not quite the same as having a meal together. It could be a new step. But before we can find out, a new obstacle appears: Sally has a date. Harry even offers advice on what she should wear: he is immediately accepting that theirs should be a friendship. It is a dance: every time they seem to be getting closer together, they are put apart again. But at this point there is at least a slight divergence between plot and emotional journeys. The plot (a big word for these small events) takes them apart, but Harry having to deal with Sally as someone involved with someone else keeps him on his emotional journey – to maturity, we might say. And it is the completion of this journey that will finally allow them to come together.

Following Sally's suggestion, Harry gets a date, too. It is a disaster. But he sleeps with the girl anyway. This capacity of his to divorce sex from feelings shows that in this area, at least, he has not changed. And it distances him from Sally.

Practising in the baseball nets with his friend, Harry refuses to accept that he wants to sleep with Sally. He seems pleased that he finally has a woman friend. He feels that he is growing (and he is). His new direction has been firmly established.

In a diner, Harry confesses to Sally that he lies to women as he leaves them after sex. This leads on to the famous fake orgasm scene, in which Sally fakes it there and then. This is very funny, of course, but it is more than that. Up to this point, Harry has been the one who has admitted to lying to people, but here is Sally showing that she can lie very convincingly, too. It is a side of her we haven't seen before (apart from one little lie when she pretended that she never forgot her friend Amanda's name). She tells Harry that she is appalled by his behaviour to women, but at the same time by this faking she is saying she is not as far from him as he thinks. What is more, she is challenging his apparent control of sexual relationships. If ever they were to have a sexual relationship, her action seems to be saying, it would be between equals.

We might pause here to comment on stylistic consistency. There are many different styles of writing for scripts. There is naturalism (or, more accurately, selective naturalism), with its attempt to be faithful to exactly how things are said and done in the 'real world', but being selective about what is shown because showing pure unedited 'slice of life' would be tedious; there is heightened naturalism, which is close to naturalism though going a little beyond it, whether in dialogue, character-isation or events themselves; and then there are various forms of non-naturalism, from surreal or absurd theatre, to varieties of Brechtian presentation, to all sorts of fantasy, from *Buffy the*

Vampire Slayer to *Austin Powers*, not to mention science fiction. All of these styles – and more – can be successful. The important thing is to be *stylistically consistent within the script*. An audience soon grasps the rules that are established early on in the production, accepts them and doesn't quibble, so long as those rules are then observed for the rest of the script. And this is what brings us back to the fake orgasm scene: in the context of the rules already established in the script, is it acceptable? Would anyone do as Sally does – fake a loud and passionate orgasm in the middle of a full diner? The answer is probably no. But as an audience we probably won't object. This is partly because we enjoy its outrageousness, and partly because we enjoy *Sally* doing it. But is she acting out of character? I would say no. Sally has always been more controlled than Harry, so we are delighted to see her, for once, acting utterly unconventionally and leaving him speechless in the process, and we might also reflect that she has not been particularly shy about talking about sex up to now, so while the action is a surprise it is not entirely lacking credibility. Sally has a point to prove, so she proves it. We know the action itself is not 'realistic', but we don't care. Some of Harry's speeches, too, are just a little too clever to be true and we don't care about that either. This is a comedy, after all, not a documentary, and it's the emotional truth that is of interest to us, not the literal truth. Within bounds, we can accept it. Of course, if this were to drift into *Monty Python* territory we might raise a few more objections.

A new sequence begins, to the song 'Winter Wonderland.' There is a series of images of people enjoying themselves in the snow. These images are mostly about people who do things together rather than separately; it is as if we are being gently reminded that Harry and Sally, too, really don't want to be alone. The sequence leads to Harry and Sally buying a Christmas tree together, an image of their togetherness in friendship. We move on to seeing them together at a New Year's party. They dance cheek to cheek, innocently. But we can see from their faces – though neither of them can see the other – that it is not innocent after all. The song here is about making two lovers from friends. They are clearly becoming closer and closer, emotionally. New Year is declared and everyone hugs – except them; it would be too dangerous. Their eyes meet at length, but each of them turns it into something else, and they give each other just a little New Year's peck. This has made things safe again, so they give each other a hug.

So, they are learning to love each other, but they refuse to admit it, certainly to each other and probably to themselves. Emotionally they have come together, but they have established rules for themselves that don't allow it to be acknowledged, certainly not to each other and possibly not to themselves. This 'possibly' is important, for we are not entirely certain what is going on in their heads. There is a continual ambiguity about what precise point they have reached, and this ambiguity along the emotional journey is one of the factors that keeps us watching: we want to sort it out, we want to have our suspicions confirmed. Of course, if a script is utterly ambiguous, and we simply don't have a clue what's going on in emotional terms, then we probably become impatient and decide that there are better ways of spending our time. But if we are *fairly but not entirely* clear about a character's position on the emotional map, this is intriguing, and being intrigued keeps us involved.

At this point, then, we are willing the protagonists to be completely honest about how far they have travelled, but they refuse.

Another interview with old people. Here we have two people totally attuned, filling in each other's sentences. The old woman talks about the moment when she knew he was the man for her. 'At that moment I knew. I knew the way you know about a good melon.' So it seems that one or both of our protagonists are ready to move on to the next stage of their emotional journey: *recognition* of where they are.

Instead of that happening immediately, however, we are given a double date, Harry matched with Sally's friend Marie, and Sally with Harry's friend Jess. But it doesn't work out as planned, as it is Marie and Jess who turn out to have things in common, and after the meal they can't wait to go off in a cab together. Here we have, so far as our protagonists are concerned, characterisation by contrast. While Sally and Harry look at things this way and that, dillying and dallying (and Harry, in particular, analysing the possibilities to a standstill), Marie and Jess just leap into a relationship together – not just sex: a relationship. The characterisation of Marie and Jess leads us to see the protagonists that much more clearly.

Another old couple. This time the old man tells us how he had not expected that the girl who had been chosen for him by his parents would be beautiful, but he found that she was, and so he married her. This, for once, is not a reference to the protagonists so much as to Marie and Jess, prefiguring *their* emotional journey. Marie had been dating a married man for years, but we have seen Sally gradually convince her that he was never going to leave his wife; meanwhile, Jess had been settling back into comfortable bachelorhood. But despite their misgivings before the double date, meeting each other instantly changed everything. They both suddenly move on into this new relationship, and into new emotional states.

While Harry and Sally are out buying a wedding present for Marie and Jess, they bump into Harry's ex-wife with her new partner. Harry cannot conceal his upsettedness. It stays with him. While they are round at Marie and Jess's who are disagreeing about furnishings, Harry is reminded of his own marriage, and yells at them about how incompatibilities like this lead inevitably to divorce. His emotional journey has taken another twist; once again he is not at all ready for a committed relationship.

Harry's outburst leads Sally to tell Harry that he must find a way not to express his every feeling, while Harry responds that Sally never seems to show upsettedness at all. This is double-edged. On the one hand it is a clear statement of the distance between them, but at the same time this *expression* of it allows growth, allows the two of them to understand each other better, and allows their journey towards each other to continue.

At a small house party, the four main characters (Harry, Sally, Jess and Marie) and friends are playing picture charades. Sally draws (badly – no-one recognises it) 'Baby Talk'. Here we have another little hint about the direction she would like to be going in. More important, she has a new boyfriend, and we see an unmistakable look of jealousy on Harry's face. But is it sexual jealousy or just jealousy over their closeness? And Harry has a new girlfriend. Sally's look of unconcern is entirely unconvincing. They are still both in denial and have placed new obstacles in their own way. And these are the first new girlfriend and boyfriend that we, the audience, have been allowed to meet. So they feel more real, and this makes them more serious, more of a threat, a greater obstacle. The closer Harry and Sally are getting, the harder they make it for themselves.

One night Sally finds out that Joe, her ex-partner, is going to get married. Despite all that she has said about being over him, she is distraught. She is finally open with her emotions, both to Harry and herself. This is a huge step forward for her. She asks Harry to come and comfort her, which he does, and this – much more through her initiative than his – leads to their finally sleeping together.

A little later, it is their respective expressions that tell us exactly the point each of them has reached. Sally is in bliss. Harry is in shock.

Now, when everything ought to be fine, nothing is. If we couldn't see this on Harry's face we should know from the music. It is a variation on 'It had to be you', except that, to start with at least, it keeps going wrong. They have finally met the biggest obstacle of all: Harry's refusal to commit himself, his fear of accepting and giving love. In the morning he leaves – if not within thirty seconds then very quickly anyway. He does ask her to have dinner with him that night – another of the invitations that act as markers in this script – but it is in the tone of an automaton: he is doing his duty.

It seems that the conflict within his head, at least, has been resolved, but not as we had expected. His journey could finish here, with the discovery that all of this had, for him, been a cul-de-sac.

At the meal each of them tells the other that it has been a mistake, but subsequently, at Jess and Marie's wedding, it becomes clear that she feels humiliated anyway. They argue violently.

Incidentally, a word on that meal. For the first time, they both eat the same thing. It is as though even while they are actually saying they should be apart they are in fact becoming more similar. And Harry's eating: at least he is not spitting out of car windows any more, but he still eats as noisily as ever. A certain amount of change, but not complete.

Another winter scene, another reference point, allowing easy comparison with the earlier scene. As Sally struggles with a Christmas tree by herself, where are we on the journey now? Sally has clearly moved a long way from the feelings she had about Harry at the start of the film, but now she both loves him and hates him. Harry, on the other hand, seems to have convinced himself that he just wants Sally as a friend, the very thing that at the outset he said was impossible.

Harry leaves a series of answerphone messages for her. She refuses to answer. The messages are ambiguous anyway. Certainly he wants to apologise, but neither she nor we are sure what sort of relationship he now wants; it is not clear what direction he wants to go in. Eventually she does answer, but makes it clear that she thinks this particular journey has finished. If he does not want to be her long-term partner, then she doesn't want to see him at all. 'I am not your consolation prize,' she tells him. She, now, refuses a non-sexual friendship. This has something in common with the position Harry started from, but is adopted for different reasons. For Harry, sex got in the way of friendships. For Sally, casual sex is not enough: it gets in the way of a serious relationship.

New Year's Eve again (another milestone). It is only towards the end of the film, and most notably here, that we hear Harry's thoughts, trying to comfort himself and failing (the music – though without the words at this point: 'They're writing songs of love, but not for me'). The stylistic consistency here might be questioned: if we are allowed to hear Harry's thoughts now, why not earlier? But we can sense we are nearing the end of the film. It is a rule broken, certainly, and yet somehow it works: it is like stepping up a gear for the final section – it adds to the sense of climax.

Sally is dancing with some man. Again there is a little characterisation by contrast. Last time we saw Sally dancing with Harry, Harry danced with wit and intelligence – it made her laugh. This man just throws her around. And similarly the conversation: where Harry is clever this man is spectacularly un-entertaining.

After intercutting between Sally at the party and Harry wandering the streets, we flash back – in Harry's head – to significant moments of the last twelve years, tracing the journey he has had. He is feeling nostalgic, of course, missing her, but we, too, are reminded of how far they have both come, and made to feel that the journey must be made to end well.

The music moves to 'It had to be you' – but now with the words heard, as Harry is allowing himself to acknowledge the sentiments – and Harry breaks into a trot, finally running for all he is worth to reach Sally before she leaves the party (and we see that she is, indeed, leaving). The running is important. It doesn't only create a sense of urgency and add to suspense – we are willing him to get to the party in time – but also, more importantly, the running is about his willingness to make an effort to make this relationship work, to show how far he has changed.

Finally, at the party, he declares his love for her. That is not enough for her – she is still too hurt – but what does break her down is a wonderful statement of how far he has come, of how he now adores those aspects of her that would once have driven him mad, and how everything about her is now part of him. This realisation is what allows them to come together, this and the fact that he has finally learned not just that it is possible to have a woman as a friend without sex getting in the way – it did get in the way, even if he didn't instigate the sex – but rather that a relationship doesn't end with sex. He has learned not to run away and – more specifically – not to run away from her. The music is Auld Lang Syne, a song, as Sally points out, about old friends.

The film ends with an interview of another married (but not very old) couple: Harry and Sally. They are looking back on their wedding. Talking about the cake, Harry accepts what Sally says, that it is important to keep the chocolate sauce on the side. They are still themselves, but *emotionally* each of them has travelled a very long way.

So, in general terms, what do we learn from this summary of the emotional journeys of these two characters?

1) The journey is of importance to them: it is not a trivial change in their feeling that takes place, but one that alters their lives.

2) They come a long way. That is not to say that they change entirely as characters – they don't – but they do go through a learning process which alters what they feel.

3) There are some clear milestones along the way, made easier to recognise by recurring events.

4) The journey has two major parts. The first is the gradual change in feelings. The second is the acknowledgement of those changed feelings.

5) The shapes of the emotional journeys are underlined through contrast with those of other characters.

6) Devices such as music, settings and other interpolated scenes – that is, *devices outside the characters themselves* – are used to help chart the progress of the emotional journeys.

7) In film (and also television and radio, it is much harder on stage) a staging post on the emotional journey can be well illustrated by a wordless sequence, often held together by music or song, or (though things are a little different on radio) the staging post may be indicated by a sequence held together by voice-over, across which we see *a series of images which taken as an entirety* portray the stage that has been reached.

8) The characters rarely state precisely where they are on the journey, and when they do they cannot be relied upon, so the audience is kept involved by doing much of the work.

9) While the general direction of the journeys is clear, there is always an element of ambiguity, of uncertainty, which keeps the audience wanting clarification.

10) The journeys are not in a straight lines: they are two steps forward, one step back.

11) There is frequent (but not inflexible) mirroring between the journeys of the protagonists. In a different script this might happen between the protagonist and the *ant*agonist.

12) The closer they get to what might be their emotional destination, the harder – emotionally – it becomes for them to reach it.

13) The length of emotional journey that has been made is acknowledged by the characters.

14) The journeys of the protagonists *reverberate*: without overstatement, attention is drawn to the fact these journeys exist in – and to some extent are representative of – a wider context of how men and women interact in general.

15) There is a false ending, where we are presented with one set of emotional endings which could have been permanent. This is an emotional might-have-been, which emphasises the achievement of the actual final destination.

The above is not a set of rules, to be applied to romantic comedy or anything else. Rather it is a set of observations about this particular script. We shouldn't set out slavishly to reproduce all these features, but just to bear in mind that these ingredients, in this case, certainly seem to have produced a script that works.

8. Description and Self-Description

From the notes we have made, we now know quite a lot about our protagonist, and we have a story in mind. But how are we actually to *show* the character? It is one thing for you, the writer, to have clarified your ideas on all sorts of aspects of this individual, but how are these aspects to be conveyed to the audience? How exactly is the audience to find out what this character is made of?

As we have seen, the most important way of showing a character is through what he or she does – the decisions that are made – but there are other ways. We also learn a great deal from what the protagonist says, of course, but we should not overlook the potential of what others say about him or her. Let us examine this last technique first, the reporting of a character.

Telling us what she's like

Take any one friend of yours – we'll call her Sandra – and ask six other people, separately, to describe that friend. Each description will be different. There will be elements that overlap, of course, but none of the descriptions will be the same. So which is the 'real' Sandra? One will say she is friendly, another that she is two-faced; one will say she is devoted to her work, another will tell you that she spends more time talking about working than actually doing it. Even basic things will be perceived very differently; one will tell you she is attractive, another that she is plain.

So, we are all seen in many different lights. Partly, of course, this is because the contexts in which we meet different people lead us to show different sides of our personality to them. People at work might only see certain sides of an individual, while family might well see someone altogether different. But even within a group who experience roughly the same side of Sandra, all at work, say, or all at the bowling club, there will be very different perceptions of her personality. This arises partly because she interacts differently with each person, but also because each person will have a different way of evaluating her, of deciding who she is. The question of which is the 'real' Sandra cannot, of course, be answered. But this fact of our all being seen in different lights by different people is very useful for the playwright: it adds depth to a character. If as audience we only see what the character shows us, then we have only that to rely upon, but if as well as this we are offered the opinions – and often conflicting opinions – of others, then we see the character in a more rounded way. It is rather like the lighting of an actor on stage. If the actor is lit by one light only, we only see one plane, and the actor looks almost unreal; if, on the other hand, the performer is lit from a number of different angles (and, better still, with coloured gels, each of which literally casts a different light) we can see the actor as a three-dimensional being. The opinions of others, then, are important in the representation of a rounded character.

Preparing the ground

We always want to establish a clear sense of *whose* story this is that we are telling, and usually it is best to do it at the start of the script. (Though there are exceptions to this as to everything else. Whose story is *Pulp Fiction*?)

One way of establishing whose story it is, is to have other characters refer to the protagonist before he or she is actually met by the audience. This focuses particular attention on the protagonist, and allows a sense of anticipation to build up, as well as giving the opportunity for background information to be imparted to the audience, so that we are then able to put the actions and words of the protagonist into context. For example, we are told of the lovelorn, dreamy Romeo (and this is not even about his relationship with Juliet, but about his angst over the previous love of his life!) before we meet him. Or, to refer to *Coriolanus* once more, at the start of that play there are over three hundred lines of discussion amongst the common people and then with Menenius, a friend of Coriolanus, before we meet the protagonist. Much of that discussion is in fact *about* Caius Martius (Coriolanus to be), his loathing of the commoners – he is described as 'chief enemy to the people' – and his extraordinary valour in war, although we are told by one citizen that he, the citizen, 'could be content to give him good report for't, but that he pays himself with being proud.' When Coriolanus then enters he immediately utters lines typical of him:

CAIUS MARTIUS [...]What's the matter, you dissentious rogues,
                That, rubbing the poor itch of your opinion,
                Make yourselves scabs?
FIRST CITIZEN   We have ever your good word.
CAIUS MARTIUS He that will give good words to thee, will flatter
                Beneath abhorring. What would you have, you curs,
                That like not peace nor war? The one affrights you,
                The other makes you proud. He that trusts to you,
                Where he should find you lions, finds you hares;
                Where foxes, geese: you are no surer, no,
                Than is the coal of fire upon the ice,
                Or hailstone in the sun.

First impressions are tremendously important in drama, as they are in life, and Shakespeare knew the truth of this. Coriolanus comes thundering into the space and immediately takes control of it, with a witheringly powerful and arrogant display of verbal muscle, reflecting not only his detestation of the people but also his own apparent invulnerability. The lines themselves are splendid; so, what would have been lost if Shakespeare had chosen to begin his play with them? Well, to some extent the lines would have been wasted; the bleatings of the citizens and the clever but relatively restrained (and humorous) put-downs of Menenius set a certain tone which is utterly overwhelmed by the mightily contemptuous lines hurled forth by Caius Martius; the impression he creates gains enormously from contrast with what has gone immediately before. More important still, though, is the fact that the *very first* impression of Coriolanus is from others. His relationship with the common people is crucial to the unfolding of events, as we have seen, so first seeing Coriolanus *through their eyes* is a vital element in establishing our perception of him.

Or, to take a more modern example, Robert Bolt's play *Vivat! Vivat Regina!* begins with a couple of maids of Mary Queen of Scots telling a lewd joke. A guest is appalled, not so much by the joke itself as by the fact that it is told by maids of the Queen who, he is sure, would be equally shocked. But the maids know their Queen: when she appears she is not the least taken aback when they offer to tell her the joke, but merely remarks that at this moment she does not have time for a 'mucky tale'. She immediately switches to formal mode to address her guest, paying due respect to the fact that he has ridden hard from France to see her. In this opening the audience is partly prepared for a somewhat bawdy Mary; the guest's reaction to the lewd joke is what we would expect of such a dignitary, and it is also what we might feel ourselves, but, like the guest, we quickly realise that the maids are, after all, right in their estimation of the Queen. Just as importantly, our surprise may spring not so much from the Queen being capable of lewdness, as from the fact of it being so openly known and acknowledged. But then the Queen's abrupt change to a formal manner of speech with her guest shows us that she is perfectly capable of performing the royal role as well. This opening has in fact presented us with a microcosm of Queen Mary's character – and the problems that will face her: she is both a highly sexual being, with much of the common touch, and at the same time perfectly regal, but the two do not sit comfortably together. And the openness of her sexuality provokes reactions – of what might be over-familiarity from the common people, and of shock from the nobility. The opening sets all this out, giving us an immediately vivid picture of the Queen's character and its context, and a major element of this is the initial *reporting* of her character.

Reporting about a character (particularly the protagonist), then, is often used near the start of a script, as part of the process of establishing the audience's perception of that character. But it has many other uses, too. At any point in a script we may have another character – perhaps quite a minor one – reminding us about a personality trait of the protagonist, maybe a trait that we might otherwise have either overlooked or forgotten, maybe a characteristic that the protagonist has attempted to leave behind, but which others have not forgotten.

And, of course, some of the opinions that characters give about each other are completely misleading. It doesn't have to be as extreme as Iago talking about Desdemona to Othello, where a series of outright lies are plainly seen to be such by the audience (indeed, Iago even takes the audience into his confidence about his lies, as though enlisting its support and understanding). Lies are one thing, where the teller knows that the words are untrue, but quite another are the opinions which are genuinely believed by the speaker and perhaps, at least for some time, by the audience, though these opinions turn out not to have been true in the end. This might be described as false characterisation, and is a very useful tool for the writer. This misleading of the audience helps us to see how the protagonist *could be seen*, and *could have been*; it also tests our own perceptiveness. Did we realise right from the start that this individual did not deserve to be spoken about in this way? In addition, false characterisation is yet another way of further involving the audience: they have to work out the true character of this person.

In Anthony Minghella's remarkable radio play *Cigarettes and Chocolate* the central character, Gemma, hardly appears. At the very start of the play we hear Gemma's answerphone, with her voice inviting people to leave messages. There follows a series of eight messages. From these we begin to construct her character. We find out a lot about who she must be from the sort of people who leave messages for her. It is not that these messages actually tell us, directly, much about her, but rather she is the space left in the middle between all these other people. It is almost as though we can tell who she is from the shape of the space. Less poetically, we learn about class, pastimes, her lover and so on. There is then a short monologue from Gemma, as though speaking her thoughts to the audience, which includes her telling us that she has stopped talking altogether. There then follows the body of the play, a series of scenes involving the friends and lover of Gemma – her best friend and boyfriend are betraying her together – but through all of this we are never in doubt that the central character is Gemma, continually referred-to, never heard. These scenes culminate in a long monologue from Lorna, her best friend, about suicide, and we sense that Gemma, too, may be contemplating this. Only at the very end of the play do we hear Gemma's thoughts once more, her overwhelming sense of the pointlessness of things, while at the same time she has found that not speaking has sharpened all her senses. She has been giving up all the things that are bad for her: last year it was cigarettes, the year before it was chocolate, and now it is words. This is a memorable speech, but is made even more so for being one of so few of hers in the whole play. She is a character successfully constructed by others.

To take a very different example, in a number of westerns Clint Eastwood appears as the Man With No Name. He is also a man with very few words. In terms of learning about him through dialogue, certainly others give their opinions about him, but he hardly utters a word about himself.

A word of warning, though, about relying too heavily upon the use of people's opinions expressed about the protagonist. For the most part, we should be learning about the character of the protagonist from what he or she *does* and says (and what the character says is not, of course, primarily expressing opinions about him- or herself!). Hearsay has its uses, as we have seen, but if the writer over-uses it then we may begin to think that there is some laziness involved. After all, it is much easier to get a secondary character to describe the traits of the protagonist than to show those characteristics through action. It is a matter of the writer choosing whether to tell or show; my advice is: when in doubt, show. Telling is always weaker. Now sometimes you want to use telling *because it is* weaker, as you want there to be doubt in the audience's mind about the truth of the account. When the audience has only been told about something, the truth of it is always in question; an audience only entirely believes what it has seen, not what it has been told about – and quite right, too.

Furthermore, an action seen is an action much more likely to be remembered. There are in fact three tiers to this: 1) what we ourselves do, 2) what we see or hear, 3) what we are told about. We are most likely to be affected by an experience (and remember it) if we are actually physically involved in it ourselves. (This is part of the attraction of presenting participatory theatre, however much it may terrify the average audience.) Second best is what we directly see or hear, and only a poor third is what we are told about. In drama we want experience to be as vivid as possible, so unless the telling is in a particularly arresting form, all other things being equal we should opt for showing rather than telling.

In *American Beauty* there is an example of where telling and showing together confirm an audience impression that turns out to have been a false one. We actually see Ricky, from the neighbours' house, repeatedly videoing Jane through the window. Jane and Angela then variously describe him as psychotic, obsessive, freakish and lunatic. We might find it hard to disagree. Yet by the end of the film Ricky has emerged as one of the most sympathetic characters, an extraordinary mixture of cool observer and warm participant in relationships. Not only the initial description but even what we have seen has set us in the wrong direction: it is the journey of the audience's opinion of the character that is then part of the interest.

There is an interesting example of character description in *Romeo and Juliet*. At the start of Act III, Mercutio describes his friend Benvolio:

MERCUTIO Thou art like one of those fellows that, when he enters the confines of a tavern, claps me his sword upon the table and says 'God send me no need of thee!' and by the operation of the second cup draws it on the drawer, when indeed there is no need.

BENVOLIO Am I like such a fellow?

MERCUTIO Come, come, thou art as hot a Jack in thy mood as any in Italy, as soon moved to be moody, and as soon moody to be moved.

BENVOLIO And what to?

MERCUTIO Nay, and there were two such, we should have none shortly, for one would kill the other. Thou? Why, thou wilt quarrel with a man that hath a hair more or less in his beard than thou hast. Thou wilt quarrel with a man for cracking nuts, having no other reason but because thou hast hazel eyes. What eye but such an eye would spy out such a quarrel? Thy head is as full of quarrels as an egg is full of meat, and yet thy head hath been beaten as addle as an egg for quarrelling. Thou has quarrelled with a man for coughing in the street, because he hath wakened thy dog that hath lain asleep in the sun...

Now, we have seen no evidence of this behaviour in Benvolio. Indeed, it is he that has been suggesting to Mercutio that they ought to take care as to where they walk and when, to avoid getting in a fight. No: this is Mercutio in fact describing *himself*, but under the guise of describing his friend. Yet for Mercutio directly to describe himself would be too blunt. Instead, Shakespeare has him wrap up his self-description as an account of another. This allows Mercutio subtly to acknowledge – but in a way that can always be denied, of course – that there is something ridiculous about his own behaviour, this unreasonable, unwarranted tendency to aggression. At the same time, through the humour, the fact that the behaviour is shown to be absurd does not diminish the pride that is felt in it. Mercutio does in fact take pride in his own ability to make a quarrel out of absolutely anything, but he knows that it must *look* absurd to others. Yet he doesn't care. This is clever characterisation by Mr Shakespeare.

Self-description

Self-description is not always as convoluted as the example just quoted. Sometimes it is much more direct. In film, television, theatre and radio there is this simple way of having the audience find out about a character: the character simply turns to the audience and tells them. Alternatively, a character may turn to another character and describe themselves to them. Both these techniques of self-description can be very effective, though both have their dangers.

If we turn again to the speech quoted on page 77, the ending of *Spend, Spend, Spend*, we will see that it is self-description of a fairly straightforward kind. Vivian is trying to be honest with herself – and with the audience – and even comes up with a fair analysis of what has happened to her. In general, when self-descriptions are simply straightforward and fairly accurate, they are in danger of being plain dull. Here, though, we are comparing notes with her. It is the end of the play. She knows what her life has been like, and we have seen it. So we are not being given this in order to *find out* about her life – we know about it already – but rather in order to see that, finally, she is coming to some sort of understanding of the link between events early in life and how one then leads the rest of it. Here, as in all the best examples of self-description, *it is not the information itself that is of primary importance, but the fact that the speaker is giving it.*

Let us take some more examples from the marvellous film written by Alan Ball, *American Beauty*. The film begins with a contemptuous description of the central character, Lester, by his daughter Jane. She loathes him, as so far as she is concerned he is not a proper father to her, but acts like an adolescent. So far, then, this perfectly fits the pattern already described: characterisation of the protagonist from the outside. But we then immediately move to a sequence held together by voice-over: Lester is speaking to the audience, while we dip in and out of scenes and images. So through the following we see suburbia from above; Lester being forced awake by an alarm clock; Lester in the shower; his wife Carolyn tending roses in the garden; the gay couple in the yard next door, watched by Lester (and we hear some of their dialogue, with each other and then with Carolyn); Jane at her computer; Carolyn rushing Lester and Jane to leave the house (we hear the dialogue here too); and finally the three of them in the car, Lester asleep in the back seat. So, filleting out Lester's voice-over monologue from the action and dialogue, it is:

> My name is Lester Burnham. This is my neighbourhood. This is my street.
> This... is my life. I'm forty-two years old. In less than a year, I'll be dead.

Of course, I don't know that yet.

And in a way, I'm dead already.

(*amused*) Look at me, jerking off in the shower.
(*then*) This will be the high point of my day.
It's all downhill from here.

That's my wife, Carolyn. See the way the handle on those pruning shears matches her gardening clogs? That's not an accident.

Man. I get exhausted just watching her.

She wasn't always like this. She used to be happy. We used to be happy.

My daughter Jane. Only child.

Janie's a pretty typical teenager. Angry, insecure, confused. I wish I could tell her that's all going to pass...

But I don't want to lie to her.

Both my wife and daughter think I'm this gigantic loser, and... they're right.

I have lost something. I'm not exactly sure what it is, but I know I didn't always feel this... sedated. But you know what? It's never too late to get it back.

This works tremendously well. Why? Firstly, it is embedded in action. Self-description without action can work (as in *Hamlet*, of course) but to make it succeed is much harder. The actions and words here are playing off each other beautifully. We are seeing and hearing his wife's highly energised behaviour, but the voice-over allows us to see it *through his eyes*. Secondly, the self-description does not present us with final conclusions: it leaves us with plenty of work to do. What has Lester lost? Is it energy, or youth, or hope, or ambition, or what? And how does he intend to get it back? Thirdly, it is intriguing: he tells us that in less than a year he will be dead. So does he have an incurable disease, leading him to know that he will be dead soon? Or is he, somehow, dead already? (In reply to his daughter's description of him, at the very start, a voice offers to kill him for her.) Fourthly, the monologue, while being a self-description, is also a statement of a *state of mind*. This is one of the most successful functions of speech direct to the audience – expressing a character's state of mind. Even the description of his wife's matching pruning shears and clogs is not essentially a description of her (though it is that as well, of course) but, more importantly, is part of his description of his own state of mind, strongly affected as it is by what his wife has become.

So, if self-description of this sort works so well, what are the dangers? The main danger, as with direct description by others, is that it can be a form of lazy writing. After all, a character's self-description is only one more opinion; the fact that someone says something about themselves doesn't make it true. We can only be sure that they are saying it, not that it is true. So self-description should normally be used to add to what we actually see and hear, not to replace it.

Worse, particularly in radio, monologue posing as self-description can be used to give a running commentary on events. This is using monologue as a way of telling us what is happening, but it is really very poor writing. On radio, the dialogue and sound effects should tell us what is happening, not monologue to the audience. Of course, speech direct to the audience can be extremely effective on radio (I use it a great deal myself), but not when it is used as a prop.

To return to *American Beauty*, later, Angela (Jane's friend) says of herself that not only does she know that she is beautiful, but she knows that any stranger seeing her would want to sleep with her. And this, she tells Jane, stops her from being ordinary, which is the worst thing that a person can be. This is very effective characterisation. The point here is not whether strangers actually do want to have sex with her as soon as they cast eyes on her, but that Angela both believes they do and likes the idea. It is the fact that she holds this opinion, rather than the truth or otherwise of the opinion itself, that builds the character. In addition, the fact that Angela is willing to tell this to Jane reveals more about her: she is proud of the effect she apparently has on men, and she is insensitive. It seems not to occur to her that in saying her attractiveness saves her from the dreaded ordinariness, she is in effect telling Jane that *she* is ordinary. Once more, the facts of the self-description are not important: the self-description tells us about the character, but not in the way the character intends. Similarly, later still, Angela tells Jane about all her sexual exploits, and how she has had sex with a famous photographer because that is how the world works. It is only much later in the film that Ricky faces her with the fact that much of what she says and does arises out of her *own fear and knowledge* of being, in fact, rather ordinary, and near the end she confesses (to Lester) that she is actually a virgin. She has moved in our eyes from being a hard, cynical, unappealing character, to being a silly but vulnerable little girl. We may have had our suspicions about her earlier, but we have been made to do some work to find out what is behind this character's self-descriptions.

9. Heroes and Villains

What is a hero and what is a villain, and do we need them? In terms of characterisation, should we be thinking in this way?

Clearly, heroes do exist in scripts and so do villains. In *Gladiator* (writers David Franzoni, John Logan and William Nicholson), for example, the great warrior and gladiator Maximus is clearly the hero, while Commodus is clearly the villain. It is a matter of morality. Maximus does little wrong (whatever qualms he may feel about having to kill so many others no more guilty then himself), while Commodus is a scheming, devious murderer, who not only dispatches his own father but attempts to seduce his own sister. In this example, then, there is little doubt. But if we move from *Gladiator* to *Coriolanus* (and there is actually much in common between the two scripts), then we find ourselves moving into an area where moral values are much less clearly defined. Is Coriolanus a hero? Certainly he is a soldier of remarkable ability and bravery, and he does what he believes is right, but does that qualify him as a hero? The answer is no. He is too deeply flawed. And besides, might it not be that heroes need villains, in order to be seen as heroes? Certainly there is no villain in *Coriolanus*, unless it is that 'many-headed Hydra', the common people. A flawed hero, then? No, Coriolanus is a flawed protagonist.

A more useful term than 'hero' is 'protagonist', and a more useful one than villain is 'antagonist.'

The strongest character

The protagonist does not need to be heroic. But he or she does need to be the central character, the character holding the script together. The protagonist needs to be *the strongest character*,

124

not in terms of morality, but in terms of interest for the audience. So the protagonist is the character with the most arresting conflicts, the most pressing choices, the strongest needs, the most involving emotional journey. Usually, it is true, the protagonist will also be in some sense 'good', or will through the course of the script become in some way 'good', but this need not always be the case. In some protagonists we may find it difficult to discern much moral good (think of *Breathless*, for example, or John Osborne's play *Look Back in Anger*), yet the identity of the protagonist is clear.

There is one other simple, rather crude fact: as audience, we almost always see more of the protagonist than any other character. It is, essentially, this person's story, so we spend time with this person. (There are exceptions to this as to everything else, of course; the example of *Cigarettes and Chocolate* is mentioned above). Our spending so much time with this character has two major effects: firstly, we finish up knowing more about him or her than anyone else in the script and, secondly, we inevitably start to identify with the character, *whatever the character is like*.

I remember that when I was working on the television series *The Bill* (in its earlier incarnation, before it became a soap opera) one of the unbreakable rules for that series was that the audience was only ever to see and hear what the police saw and heard. Clearly, this was a severe limitation. It meant that the opportunities for dramatic irony (having the audience know more than the characters) were severely limited. It reduced the options for creating suspense, too. We could never show the villains planning a robbery, say, or scheming to avoid capture, because the police have a tendency not to be present on such occasions, and if they weren't present we couldn't show it. So, given the major drawbacks, why did the production team insist upon this ordinance? The reason was, they wanted the audience to see the events *from the police point of view*, first literally and then, as result, psychologically. If we arrive with the police (a hand-held camera following the officer into the room) and see and hear only what they see and hear, and leave with the police, then we almost start to think of ourselves as police, as we ask ourselves, 'What would I do?' in whatever situation is presented.

The 'I' in the question is 'I' as a police officer. It is their chat that we hear, their conflicts which involve us, their actions that we are privy to. We become one of them, so we identify with them.

This is an extreme example, but the principle holds: *if we are long enough in the company of a character, we will tend to identify with that character*. This holds true even when the character has obvious major flaws (as Coriolanus does). If we are made to see the world through the eyes of a character, then some degree of identification will follow.

There are, however, limits. We should draw a distinction here between moral worth and likeability. John Becker, for example, in the television series of that name, is bad-tempered and rude, does not suffer fools gladly and is often selfish. He could never be called a hero. But while his faults are obvious, he is at the same time likeable. He has a fairly well-hidden caring side, is actually emotionally vulnerable (despite the exterior) and has a strong sense of humour. We enjoy his company, and even find ourselves delighting in his political incorrectness. All of this has very little to do with morality: we enjoy his company because we like him, and this allows audience identification.

This leads us on to the 'anti-hero'. This is the protagonist/ hero who is in fact bad. There is a very long tradition of such figures. Over three hundred years ago Ben Jonson was creating wonderful anti-heroes such as Face and Subtle in *The Alchemist* and Volpone and Mosca in *Volpone*. These are rogues of such wit (in both senses) and ingeniousness, and those they swindle are so staggeringly idiotic, that we willingly lend them our support. What they are doing is wrong in a way that is much clearer than anything Becker might get up to, but we don't much care. The world is put to rights in the end, of course, with tricks unmasked, but the fact that some of these characters are punished does not turn them into villains. Apart from entertaining us, they have exposed both hypocrisy and stupidity, and through that we have identified with them. We cannot now simply categorise them as villains.

If, on the other hand, there is little or nothing to like in the protagonist – or, worse, in any of the other characters in the script either – then no matter how well constructed the script, how well thought-through the conflicts and the choices, there will be little audience identification. When working as a script reader I remember writing on more than one report, 'I simply don't like any of these characters.' A report that included that sentence was fairly damning. Perhaps the world shouldn't be like this, but I believe it is. As audience, we need to find something we like in our protagonist, something attractive. Maybe it is a cleverness with words, or an endearing physical trait, or unexpected moments of softness. But something.

This said, there are scripts which have been produced in which virtually none of the characters shows any redeeming features. For me, the film *Looking for Mr Goodbar* (writer, Richard Brooks) falls into this category. Perhaps there are some audiences who find unattractiveness attractive, I don't know. But I lose interest in this film (and other similar productions) and neither the frequent sex scenes nor the melodrama come near to compensating for the unattractiveness of the characters: I cease to care about these people, so I cease to care about the whole production.

This brings us to why audience identification is important in the first place. It is a major means of getting the audience to *care* about what happens to the characters – just as they would care about what happens to themselves. This means we want to know what happens next. This means we don't turn off, walk out or go down to the pub instead. So it is quite important.

Antagonists

The antagonist can be an out-and-out villain, a Commodus, or Howard Payne in the film, *Speed*. In this case it is unlikely that he or she will be a straightforwardly attractive character, but the antagonist should *fascinate*. It is this fascination that should lead us to want to know what happens next to this character. We want the villain to get what he or she deserves; we keep watching to make sure it happens.

We should remember that an audience needs to be as clear about the motivation of the villain as about that of the protagonist. Generally, the villain should thoroughly believe in his or her actions, not that they are necessarily right in a conventional sense, but that they conform to a private moral code, which may be an inversion of the conventional one or may be something else altogether. An excellent example is Edmund, in *King Lear*. An illegitimate son of the Earl of Gloucester, and thus half-brother to the legitimate son Edgar, he rails at what he sees as the injustice of being born second-class, and will follow only what he sees as some form of natural law – the survival of the most unscrupulous – rather than any normal law of the land:

> Thou, Nature, art my goddess; to thy law
> My services are bound. Wherefore should I
> Stand in the plague of custom, and permit
> The curiosity of nations to deprive me?
> For that I am some twelve or fourteen moonshines
> Lag of a brother? Why bastard? Wherefore base?
> When my dimensions are as well compact,
> My mind as generous and my shape as true
> As honest madam's issue? Why brand they us
> With base? With baseness, bastardy? Base, base?
> Who in the lusty stealth of nature take
> More composition and fierce quality
> Than doth within a dull stale tired bed
> Go to the creating a whole tribe of fops
> Got 'tween asleep and wake? Well, then,
> Legitimate Edgar, I must have your land.
> Our father's love is to the bastard Edmund
> As to the legitimate. Fine word, 'legitimate'!
> Well, my legitimate, if this letter speed
> And my invention thrive, Edmund the base
> Shall to the legitimate. I grow, I prosper:
> Now gods, stand up for bastards!

Here is a full explanation of Edmund's actions. The source of what becomes his evil is embedded in his resentment of having been born out of wedlock, and the utterly unfair treatment that he feels he has received – along with all the labels – as a result of this. This is a villain who believes that what he is doing is justified. We understand his motivation. Yet he is a more interesting villain than even this implies, as a little later not only does he acknowledge his own wickedness, but he specifically denies that he is bad just as a result of circumstance (or, as he puts it, because of the star he was born under).

> This is the excellent foppery of the world, that when we are sick in fortune, often the surfeits of our own behaviour, we make guilty of our disasters the sun, the moon and the stars, as if we were villains on necessity, fools by heavenly compulsion; knaves, thieves and treachers by spherical predominance; drunkards, liars and adulterers by an enforced obedience of planetary influence; and all that we are evil in by a divine thrusting on. An admirable evasion of whoremaster man, to lay his goatish disposition to the charge of a star. My father compounded with my mother under the dragon's tail and my nativity was under Ursa Major; so that it follows I am rough and lecherous. Fut! I should have been that I am had the maidenliest star in the firmament twinkled on my bastardising.

There is a contradiction here. If his actions are justified, why are they wicked? It is a contradiction which – even if we are only half aware of it – fascinates us. He knows there are reasons – or justifications – for what he does and yet, unlike weaker villains, he wants to take full responsibility for his actions. He has no wish to blame them on anyone or anything else. And, despite what he actually does, it is hard not to feel some admiration for this figure. He takes a pride in what he is. This is an out-and-out villain, certainly, but a complex one.

This speech from Edmund, in fact, raises a major issue within characterisation, which has been touched upon – particularly with reference to *Spend, Spend, Spend* – but not directly dealt with. It is the issue of free will and environmental influences. A really successfully drawn major character will have shown these two in balance. We want to show that the character has to a large extent been formed by the influences he or she has been exposed to, but if we are only the sum of our influences then surely free will cannot exist. Yet most of us believe in free will, and certainly the characters we create must exert their will, must be making choices on the basis of that free will. We as writers are rather like barristers in court: if we want our characters to take credit or blame for what they do, we emphasise free will, while if we want them not to have to take full responsibility, we emphasise the influences to which they have been exposed, usually through no fault of their own. For the writer, this is not a matter of how we create a character, in the sense of the planning, but is a matter of how we present the character. In general, the more background we present, the more we will understand the actions of the character, and the more sympathetic we will be. (Incidentally, there is a wonderful moment in *Robin Hood, Prince of Thieves*, written by Pen Densham and John Watson, when the outrageous Sheriff of Nottingham for a moment tries to excuse his actions to an incredulous Maid Marian by referring to his supposedly terrible childhood. He is, of course, making an apparent attempt to play upon her good nature, except that the attempt is so brief, feeble and patently insincere that he must realise it is bound to fail. So it functions as a joke. It is like a writer's wink to the audience, via the character, as though to say, 'If you think you're going to get Character Formation for this evil creature, you can think again.')

To return briefly to the other (and in most ways very different) example referred to above, *Speed* (writer, Graham Yost): here again we have a clever villain, Howard Payne. While he may not feel the need to philosophise about whether or not he was destined to be evil, he certainly is provided with strong motivation for what he does. Again, Payne has developed an obsession (like many villains), believing that what he is doing is justified, even if it is outside the conventional moral code. The plot is a simple one. Payne is attempting to extort money by threatening to destroy first an elevator car and then (for most of the film) a bus; the final showdown is on a train. The hero, Jack Traven (he is a hero), is naturally trying to stop him and to save as many lives as possible. The two super-objectives, then, are in complete opposition. The whole piece, including the polar opposition, is totally contrived, but we probably don't complain. If we're going to go and see a film like *Speed* we can't be expecting High Art; we go expecting lots of action and suspense, and this is what we get. If the characterisation of our hero is somewhat thin – he is brave, intelligent and passably charming, but we know little more about him – then the compensation is that the motivation of the villain (splendidly played by Dennis Hopper) is spelt out with clarity. He is an aggrieved, disabled ex-policeman who believes himself to have been mistreated. (This is also, incidentally, a good example of back-story informing the characterisation.) In *Speed* the villain is, in fact, by far the more compelling of the two characters, but we know what sort of a film it is so we don't want to become attached to him – we know he is going to come to a grizzly end. Payne is not, of course, at all nice, but he is fascinating. And there is a wonderful tongue-in-cheekness about his repeated taunting, 'What do you do?' as he poses Jack with each new awful choice. (Again this is like a grim little joke from writer to audience, via the character, almost as if the writer were turning to us and saying, 'This is how this sort of script is constructed: you make your protagonist take massive decisions – "What do you do?" – and then he has to live with the consequences.') The hero-and-villain scenario is about good and evil, and in *Speed* the categories are very firmly drawn.

But not all antagonists are villains. An antagonist is simply the character who continually gets in the way of the protagonist achieving his or her goal. The antagonist can come in all sorts of guises. In *True West*, an unusual play in many respects, the two brothers are the dual protagonists and also dual antagonists: each stands in the way of the other's goal. And in a thousand other scripts there are a thousand other types of antagonists: they are whoever or whatever gets in the way. In many of these scripts there is, in fact, no single clear antagonist at all. To take examples that we have already looked at, who is the antagonist in, say, *Spend, Spend, Spend* or *Coriolanus*? There are no single clear antagonists in these scripts. In *American Beauty* Lester is clearly the protagonist and perhaps his wife Carolyn is the antagonist, but that is too simplistic. Certainly she stands in the way of his new aim of achieving some sort of freedom, but then perhaps that aim is unattainable anyway. And it is not Carolyn who thwarts him by killing him, but his neighbour the Colonel. In fact, protagonists come across a variety of obstacles to achieving their aims, and these obstacles often arise out of a combination of factors – including opposing elements within themselves, as Boal points out. It is often assumed that central characters are either protagonist, on the one hand, or antagonist, on the other, but in my view this is altogether too schematic. The identity of the protagonist is often – but not always – clear. Frequently, though, it is hard to pin down who *the single* antagonist might be.

For simplicity, I have been speaking about 'the protagonist', meaning the central character, but we should be aware that in most scripts there are actually a number of central characters. One of them may be *the* protagonist, but in fact there are many personal journeys being traced. All of these protagonists have antagonists. These antagonists are not necessarily enemies, of course, but they are individuals (or sometimes things) that separately or combined stand in the way of the protagonists achieving their respective objectives. In fact, a central character that we might consider a protagonist may at the same time be the antagonist to another central character, and so on. Real scripts are rarely as straightforwardly schematised as some commentators would have us believe.

10. Secondary and Minor Characters

Many inexperienced writers pay a great deal of attention to characterisation of major characters, but then only sketch in the secondary and minor ones. This is a mistake. Secondary and minor characters are important, and all but the most insignificant of roles should be constructed with a great deal of care. It is perhaps unrealistic to suggest that all characters – including the one-line doorman or passenger steward – should be given the same attention as the protagonist, but certainly this should apply to supporting secondary (as opposed to minor) characters. If the secondary characters are unconvincing, they threaten the credibility of the whole script. But we can be more positive: secondary and minor characters can add hugely to the impact of the completed work.

In general, secondary characters should amplify the themes of the script and *throw light on the characterisation of the central characters*. There are a number of ways in which this can be achieved. One is by offering alternatives, showing another path that the protagonist might have taken. In the film *Secrets and Lies* (writer, Mike Leigh), for example, Hortense is trying to find the identity of her birth mother (who turns out to be one of the other main characters, Cynthia), who had her adopted immediately after she was born. Hortense chats with her friend Dionne:

> DIONNE   [...] I did something really bad.
> HORTENSE Oh, no, I don't think I can deal with no confessions.
> DIONNE   Cleanse my soul!
> HORTENSE Mm – mm!
> DIONNE   I did the do!

HORTENSE   Do it!
DIONNE   Did the deed!
HORENSE   Did it!
DIONNE   With a complete stranger.
HORTENSE   No – what?
DIONNE   Dunno. (*She giggles*)
HORTENSE   Well what did 'e look like?
DIONNE   Dunno. 'E was in advertising.
HORTENSE   (*West Indian accent*) Oh, Lard!
(*They laugh.* HORTENSE *buries her head in her arm. Normal voice:*)
Did you use a condom?
DIONNE   Yes.
HORTENSE   Did you use two?
DIONNE   Yes.
HORTENSE   One on top of the other?
DIONNE   One after the other.
HORTENSE   Oh, God!
DIONNE   (*Laughing*) D'you despair of me?
HORTENSE   (*Looking at her*) No.
DIONNE   Yes, you do.
HORTENSE   I don't. Did you 'ave a good time?
DIONNE   Yeah.
HORTENSE   That's all that matters, then, innit?
DIONNE   Yeah.

Then a little later on, Dionne talks about how, since her mother has apparently made little effort with her, and her father has left the home, she doesn't want either of them to know much about her.

We see nothing more of Dionne in the film, so why did Leigh bother to introduce her? What does she add?

First of all, she gives a social setting to Hortense. For much of the film we see Hortense first nervously looking for her mother and then, once she has found her, trying hard to be comfortable with a person very different from herself. But here the conversation with her friend, and particularly those parts of it that are initiated by her friend, show a different side of her, relaxed and easy-going. Secondly, Hortense is black and Dionne is black. Except for the very opening of the film, at the funeral of her adopted mother, attended by almost entirely black mourners, we see Hortense in the company of white people, as her birth mother turns out to be white. So it is important that we see her with this black friend, re-emphasising her comfortable position within black society.

In addition, Dionne throws light on both Hortense and Cynthia. The light she throws upon Hortense is by contrast. Dionne has been irresponsible, and this has the effect of emphasising Hortense's generally responsible attitude. And in particular Dionne wants to be rid of her parents, as Hortense so easily could, but instead Hortense is going to great lengths to try to find her birth parents. In Dionne we are shown something like an alternative Hortense, with the choices she could have made.

Dionne throws even more light upon Cynthia (who, of course, she has never met). We later learn that many years ago Cynthia had casual sex with a man who she can hardly even remember: this turns out to have been Hortense's father. In those days, of course, having an illegitimate baby was a great disgrace, and when reminded of it – and on realising who the father must have been – Cynthia is deeply ashamed. But if we think back to Dionne's speech, and Hortense's accepting attitude towards her actions, we are liable to pass a much less harsh judgement on Cynthia than she passes upon herself.

For a rather different example, let us turn once more to *Pretty Woman*. The protagonists are, of course, millionaire businessman Edward Lewis and prostitute Vivian Ward; three minor characters throw particularly significant light upon them. These are Vivian's friend and prostitute colleague Kit de Luca, Edward's friend and business colleague Philip Stuckey, and Mr Thompson, the Hotel Manager. Kit presents us with an alternative Vivian (like Vivian, though, a somewhat idealised prostitute). The magnitude of Vivian's decision to refuse Edward's offer to make her a kept woman is made clear through Kit's astonishment. After all, this was an offer that could have utterly changed the lifestyle of someone like Kit – or Vivian. This in turn emphasises how far Vivian has already changed. Then at the end Kit, at least for the moment, is staying in prostitution, while Vivian has decided to get out of it. Through Kit we can see how easy it could be to stay, and so we respect Vivian's decision even more. Similarly, Stuckey throws light on Edward. The very fact that this man is apparently Edward's best friend says a great deal about Edward: Stuckey is fairly repulsive, and concerned only for money. Then the way Stuckey relates to Vivian also throws light upon Edward. Stuckey does not treat her as a person to be respected at all once he finds out that she is a prostitute, but only abuses and then attempts to use her. Edward's generally respectful attitude is thrown into sharp relief. And finally the Hotel Manager is a beautifully drawn character, dignified yet not aloof, compassionate yet not lenient. His function is not to throw light through contrast with the protagonists but instead by mirroring them. Like Edward, he is from the start patient and respectful towards Vivian, and like him too, increases his regard for her as the film progresses. Edward's respect for her is, in a sense, validated. The Hotel Manager has a plot function, delicately allowing Edward to find Vivian at the end of the film, but his other functions are more important. His relationship with Edward is a slight one, but ends with a lovely touch: Edward had never bothered to remember his name, Mr Thompson, but in the final hotel scene he uses it. This is not merely a statement of some sort of unacknowledged understanding between them (though it is that, too); it also acts as a gentle revelation of how much Vivian has changed Edward: the old Edward could not be bothered to remember the names of hotel employees, but the new Edward has been fully humanised.

All of these are fully rounded characters, behind which we can sense complete lives, though we are given only glimpses. They have their own ways of speaking, dressing, thinking and relating. They are not merely fill-ins, but do succeed in telling us a great deal about the characters. *They also have their own journeys*. These may not be as complete or as meaningful as those of the central characters, but they exist nevertheless. Not every secondary character can be said to have their own journey depicted through the script, but usually they do, and this always adds greatly to their own depth and to their capacity to shed light on the central characters.

There are some secondary or minor characters, though, who do *not* reflect directly upon the protagonists. Very often these are unusual or even strange individuals, whose only function appears to be to remind us that the world does have many unusual and strange people in it. The Coën brothers delight in peppering their scripts with such individuals. In *The Big Lebowski*, for example, secondary characters include a leather-clad nihilist, a legless high achiever also named Lebowski, an aggressive paedophile bowler with 'Jesus' on his shirt, a Stranger dressed as a cowboy (who turns out to be the narrator), a man with an iron lung and three individuals who appear to be Nazis, but feeble ones. These minor characters do not reflect directly upon the protagonists, but create *a world* for this particular script, a world peopled by extreme individuals. If they reflect on the protagonists (who themselves are hardly average people) then it is only to make them appear rather more normal, since everyone in the world of this script is in some way extraordinary.

This leads us on to a general point: every script in fact creates its own world. The world of Oscar Wilde's *An Ideal Husband*, say, is very different from that of *American Beauty*, which is very different again from that of *Spend, Spend, Spend*. The most important distinguishing feature of each of these different worlds is not really the setting (upper-class London, suburban America, northern English town), nor the period, but is *its relationship to naturalism*. Naturalism, that attempt to reproduce life exactly 'as it is' has been played with in a million different ways, or rather the thing itself – life exactly 'as it is' – has been played with. It is heightened in various ways, or even deliberately subverted. There are any number of approaches to the presentation of reality, each creating its different world (or different perception of reality) but, as has been noted previously, what is most important for the writer is consistency of approach in creating this world. It is here that secondary characters are of great importance: they reinforce the *world* of the script. Thus in *The Big Lebowski* we have major characters who are all idiosyncratic and events that are exceptional, but then the secondary characters make it clear that these central characters exist in a world in which the idiosyncratic and apparently exceptional are actually the norm. It is a view of the world that casts every individual as eccentric in their own way.

All this said, however, it is still the case that each minor character should be there for a reason. He or she should have a function within the plot, or should be supporting, mirroring or offering an alternative to one of the central characters. But then they shouldn't *only* be seen in terms of their plot function. Every individual, however small the role, should be distinctive, with their own colouring. Because real people are.

11. The Comic Character

Many characters are comic as well as serious. Adding comedy to a character or, rather, adding an ability to make people laugh (rather than being unconsciously comic), adds depth to the character and also makes him or her more attractive. Riggs in the *Lethal Weapon* series, for example, is both serious and funny (less serious and more funny in each film progressively). The combination is a winning one.

Here, however, I am concerned with characters who are *essentially* comic. Comic characters can, of course, be either central characters or minor ones, but if a central character is comic then the script is a comedy, whereas a minor character can be comic in any type of script, including serious drama. To try to have an essentially comic character as one of the central players in a serious drama would lead to an incongruity: major comic characters bring with them an essentially comic world, which it is very difficult for major serious characters to inhabit.

Comedy and naturalism

In general, comedy tends to be further from naturalism than other dramatic forms. This is because, in order to produce comic effects, we are very often stretching reality, taking something that the audience recognises and then exaggerating it to the point where the absurdity that lies at its core is revealed. So comic characters tend to be at some distance from naturalism.

There are, however, many exceptions. One does not need to exaggerate the speech of many loquacious and proudly commonsensical cab drivers to make it funny. 'I had that [add any famous name] in the back of my cab, you know... ' has become a cliché, but only because so many cab drivers actually say it, so when we put this line into our script it is immediately funny while being entirely naturalistic. There are many other clichéed characters – the pompous school teacher, the smarmy political aide and so on – which raise a smile as soon as they appear. The problem is, they usually do little more than raise a smile, as these cardboard characterisations are too used and tired. To be really successful we need to *play with the cliché*. The cabbie can be transposed onto the Thames as a sixteenth-century ferryman. When *he* turns to his passengers (as he does in *Shakespeare in Love*, written by Marc Norman and Tom Stoppard) and tells them that he has had so-and-so in the back of his boat, then that is indeed funny.

Much of the humour here derives from recognising a *character type*. A similar form of humour arises simply from recognising the traits of a particular individual, rather than a type. This works best in series, as we have the most opportunity over a period to know the characters' foibles, but it can also be successful in single free-standing scripts. I remember when I first watched an episode of the television comedy series *Frasier* I didn't find it funny at all. But I was told to persevere, so I watched it again. I was soon in stitches. I realise now that much of the humour only really works once the audience knows these characters, as the lines are not so much intended by the characters to be funny (though there are also a fair number of these) as intended by the characters to be serious, but found funny by the audience because they are so typical of that particular character. So when Niles utters some pathetic lines intended to bolster his frail ego, or makes some gesture which betrays his unexpressed yearning for Daphne (before they destroy each other's marriages) then we are very soon laughing, as these are *so Niles*. The same applies to Ros letting slip another sexual misadventure, or Marty being solidly down-to-earth, or Frasier himself being a snob yet not realising it. The lines may or may not be funny in themselves, but it is the broader characterisation that is fundamental to the success of this type of humour.

Humour tinged with sadness

Many comic characters are also in some sense sad. When we create a character who is both funny and at the same time pathetic, the combination can be very moving. In *Steptoe and Son* (writers, Alan Simpson and Ray Galton) Harold Steptoe makes continual pathetic attempts to show that he is really of a higher class than one might assume of a rag-and-bone man. He tries to become acquainted with The Arts and to talk posh. He fails at both, sometimes realising that he is failing, other times managing to fool himself. But we are not fooled for a moment, and while his attempts are funny they are also sad. The combination produces both empathy and sympathy. Harold's father, too, is not taken in by his son's attempts to be something he is not, but he is pathetic in his own way, too, for whenever his son has some chance of escaping to a better life the old man thwarts it. He is pathetically holding on to his son, because he has nothing else. And for all his attempts to change things, ultimately Harold only has his father, too. As the saying goes: if it weren't so funny it would be tragic.

This leads us back to a category of comic character which we have touched upon earlier: the deluded. Harold harbours delusions of social superiority. Being deluded about one's own position in the world is a major source of comedy in general. In Ben Jonson's play *Volpone*, for example, we are given Lady Would-be, who likes to think she is a great source of knowledge on any subject, as well as being the most wonderful company:

LADY WOULD-BE   Come, in faith, I must
Visit you more days; and make you well:
Laugh, and be lusty.
VOLPONE   My good angel save me!
LADY WOULD-BE There was but one sole man in the world,
With whom I could ere sympathize; and he
Would lie you often, three, four hours together
To hear me speak: and be, sometime, so rapt,
As he would answer me, quite from the purpose,

> Like you, and you are like him, just. I'll dis-
> course,
> And't be but only, sir, to bring you asleep,
> How we did spend our time, and loves,
> together,
> For some six years.
>
> VOLPONE   Oh, oh, oh, oh, oh.

The humour here arises out of Lady Would-be deluding herself, and our reading between the lines. *Reading between the lines* is in fact a frequent source of humour, where a character means us to understand one thing but we can see that the truth is quite different, because this is a character with delusions. In this example, then, Lady Would-be means us to understand that her listener was enthralled, when we realise he must have been utterly bored and desperate to escape; she thinks he was so enraptured that this somehow took his thoughts elsewhere, so that he would comment on some quite different topic, when in fact we can see that in his boredom he was probably no longer even listening. Then when she mentions helping Volpone to relax and sleep, we can only too easily imagine that she must have experienced sending people to sleep many times before.

Lady Would-be also serves as an example of an obsessive (Jonson's plays are littered with them). Just as many villains are obsessives, allowing one thought to so dominate the mind that the whole personality is criminally distorted, so many comic characters, too, are obsessive, but here the obsession only renders them ridiculous, which allows us to laugh at them. We might wish to make a distinction here between characters we want the audience to *laugh at* and those we want the audience to *laugh about*. In general, if we laugh about a character we will be able to be more sympathetic to that character, while if we are continually laughing directly at a character then that process will have a distancing effect. It will be hard to sustain a central comic character if we are mainly laughing at that character, as this inhibits audience identification, which is just as important in comedy as in other forms.

Many minor comic characters are two-dimensional, but we do not object to that. If their function is purely to amuse and they succeed then we don't complain. Some of them are in fact only there to give human embodiment to a running gag. This usually consists of a repeated line or action, which is developed slightly each time. The standard number of occurrences is three (set-up; establish as repeated gag; give a tweak) but some gags are repeated over and over again. In this case the reference to the line or action usually becomes more and more brief, so that the audience eventually is laughing at merely the slightest hint of the gag itself. In such circumstances, we are not dealing with in-depth characterisation, but rather with whatever surface image of character is necessary to make the gag work.

In comedy the *gallery of characters* that is created is especially important. It is important in all drama, of course, as there should be all the necessary characters to allow them to work off each other, and particularly to highlight the characteristics of the central characters. In comedy, though, there is an extra element to be considered, as status is such a rich mine of comic relationships. If you supply your central characters with other characters who have very clear status relationships with them, you are then providing endless opportunities for humour, as all the various forms of master-servant/superior-inferior relation-ship – and the subverting of them – allow status gaps to be exploited as an endless source of fun. A recent twist on the master-servant relationship occurs in the film *A Life Less Ordinary* (writer, John Hodge): Robert, the kidnapper, should be the master, but instead it is Celine, the kidnap victim, who actually manages to call the shots. In fact any number of comedies, from *Sergeant Bilko* to *Upstairs, Downstairs* to *Blackadder*, have status relationships at their core. Building in a gallery of characters that allows their fullest exploration is a wise move for the writer of comedy.

One final note. Certainly there are many fine scripts in which the characters display dazzling verbal dexterity which both amazes and amuses us (the plays of Tom Stoppard come to mind). Nevertheless, in many of the best comedies, comic characters do not *set out* to be funny. They are funny despite themselves and very often without knowing it, as frequently other characters do not acknowledge the humour – it is left to the audience to do that. So you don't have to create characters who tell jokes. Quite possibly you don't even have to create characters who are spontaneously witty. Rather, you have to create characters who, when placed in certain situations, *become funny to the audience*. That is what is important.

12. Leaving your characters

There are two senses in which I want to talk about leaving your characters. The first is leaving your characters as you want them to be, so that you are satisfied with them.

Imagine: you have thought of your idea for a script, you have done the research, you have created the characters, you have written the script. But at the end of all this, there is still a character who doesn't work. What do you do? The first thing, of course, is to try to identify the problem. Does the character not have sufficient conflict? Is motivation unclear? Are we told too much but not shown enough? Is the character not sufficiently contextualised (think of how useful that scene was, between Hortense and Dionne in *Secrets and Lies*)? Is the backstory unconvincing? What is it?

If you can identify the problem, then naturally you deal with it as best you can, but I suggest that when you feel a character really isn't working, don't tinker. Make wholesale changes. And if these don't rectify the problem, just experiment – but experiment in a big way (though always keeping your precious drafts, of course). Be radical. Try changing the gender. This will have a huge knock-on effect right through the script – you will find all sorts of things are altered. But do it anyway. If it isn't the solution it might at least lay bare what the solution could be. Or change the character's age, or possibly even his or her race. Or make major alterations to the character's background. Failing that, it may actually be that the plot is not allowing the character to develop properly: it may not be character as such that is the problem, but rather the scope for emotional journey. Again, if this is the case don't just tinker with the plot: re-work it.

And don't be content with a character that doesn't work, or only partially works. Don't think no-one will notice. They will.

Finally, there is the second sense of leaving your character. Just as initial impressions are extremely important, so are last impressions. It is a matter of symbolism, or characterisation by association. If, for example, whenever we meet a particular character it is always in murky alleyways, we will start to feel that this character, too, is murky. If we only ever meet a character in cheap yet ostentatious surroundings, then this character will start to feel cheap and pretentious too. Similarly language can perform this function. Shakespeare was very fond of associating certain characters with certain recurring images – of blood, for example: unconsciously, the connection is made.

So symbolism and imagery are important tools of characterisation, and never more so than at the end. The moment when the audience last sees or hears a character should be chosen carefully, as it is one of the moments that will stick in the mind. The last that we see of Harry Lime in the film of *The Third Man* (writer, Graham Greene) is his fingertips. We view them from street level, as desperately, from below, he is clawing at a grill. If he can get it open he just might escape. We see the fingertips, and then we see them go limp and slip back down through the grill. We know he has died. This man who a little earlier had been literally up in the sky, looking down with a mixture of indifference and contempt at the dots of humanity below, has slipped back into the interminable network of subterranean tunnels and sewers, where it is appropriate that this devious, scheming man should now lie. We are never shown his dead body: the grasping, then finally limp fingers are much more eloquent.

The last we see or hear of a central character should be memorable, an image worthy of the character you have created.

Index